Abbott Fay

Famous Coloradans

124 People Who Have Gained Nationwide Fame

Mountaintop Books
1750 Highway 133
Paonia, CO 81428
(303) 527-3120

First Edition.

Produced with the support of the Colorado Endowment for the Humanities, Denver, Colorado, a grantee of the National Endowment for the Humanities.

Library of Congress Number 90-60302

ISBN 0-9625850-0-9

Contents

The Preventers and Healers   1

The Scientists   9

The Naturalists   17

The Music Makers   25

The Entertainers   35

The Story Tellers   47

The Poets   65

The Picture Makers and Stone Carvers   73

The Teachers   87

The Planners and Builders   97

The Merchants   109

The Union Leaders   117

The Lawyers   123

The Political Leaders   129

The Defenders 141

The Spacemen 147

The Athletes 153

The Holiday Maker 161

The Record Keepers 165

Acknowledgments and Bibliography173

Index 179

Preface

The word *famous* is an arbitrary term. Someone who is famous from the viewpoint of one observer may be totally unknown or of minor significance in the experience of another. The writer was forewarned by more than one historian that such an undertaking as listing "Famous Coloradans" would be fraught with controversy, to say the least. The inclusions here represent only 124 individuals from among nearly 200 who were considered by the writer or recommended by others.

For that reason, it would be appropriate to establish the main standards for inclusion. In the first place, the individual must have attained national or international fame in his or her field of endeavor, no matter how renowned he or she may have been in Colorado or the American West. The individual must have been born in Colorado or have spent at least five years engaged in the activity for which fame was attained while a resident of this state. (Most were not born in Colorado.) Famous people who spent only summers in Colorado or eventually retired here were not usually included. There have been some rare exceptions to these guidelines, but they served as a rule of thumb. The many infamous characters who romped through Colorado history have been omitted from this work, although not all of the inclusions were especially heroic. According to the dictionary, heroes must possess a "nobility of spirit" in their attainments. That calls to mind the inflation of terminology such as a recent poll showing that American teenagers voted actor Tom Cruise as the greatest American hero or a *Time* magazine cover proclaiming actor Kevin Costner as the "New American Hero." To be famous does not mean one has to be heroic, by any means.

Selection is most difficult in the field of athletics, since there are so many achievers given so much publicity, sometimes for only a short time. As artist Andy Warhol once said, everyone can be famous for fifteen minutes. However, it is true that Colorado has produced more noted athletes, especially in the winter sports, than its population would indicate. For that reason, inclusions here are somewhat symbolic. Some have not had the chance to stand the test of historical perspective.

Another attainment which becomes delicate is in the field of business or accumulation of wealth. It seems that names such as Coors or Gates were included because they had their names on products, while Jesse Schwayder was not nationally recognized because he used the sensible trade name of "Samsonite."

In addition to the lengthy acknowledgments at the end of the book, the writer wishes to thank the Colorado Endowment for the Humanities for its support in making possible the research and preparation of this biographical study of "Famous Coloradans."

Abbott Fay
Paonia, 1990

Notes:

Unless place names are accompanied by state designations, they are all Colorado towns, cities or regions.

Boldface personal names designate persons whose biographies appear elsewhere in this study.

Within each section, the subjects are arranged in alphabetical order. No attempt has been made to rank their greatness.

The Preventers and Healers

A Founder of Social Medicine ...
Richard W. Corwin

Some called Richard Corwin a genius. He was not only a nationally recognized expert on trauma surgery, hospital administration, and industrial medicine, but was one of the first in the nation to recognize that "physical, mental and moral development go hand in hand," working to improve the conditions of men and their families through his sociological department at the Colorado Fuel and Iron Hospital in Pueblo. Corwin was also a world traveler, archaeologist, ornithologist, and an avid collector of oddities, such as shrunken heads and rare artifacts of ancient civilizations.

A native of New York, Corwin was born in 1852 and worked his way through Cornell University as a taxidermist. He went on to Medical School at the University of Michigan, where he served as curator of the University Museum to earn his way, getting his MD degree in 1878. After his residency, he went to Pueblo to serve as physician for the Colorado Fuel and Coal Company, a company with a tiny hospital. Commissioned to plan a greater hospital, he travelled extensively to study successful facilities. His new hospital became a national model of efficiency and cheerful atmosphere. His efforts to teach the foreign-born better health practices gained him additional fame.

He had already retired from the National Guard when World War I broke out, but he went to Europe with the Rockefeller Institute to help in battlefield treatment and development of new curative methods, winning a decoration from the Queen of Belgium.

Richard Corwin was a civic leader, serving the Pueblo school board for forty years. He was also president of the Colorado Medical Society in 1901 and 1902. He never married. When he died in 1929, Puebloans renamed their famous hospital for him.

A Real Cavity Fighter . . .

Frederick S. McKay

Frederick McKay was a Colorado Springs dentist who noted that some of his patients from a nearby region had a distinctive discoloration of their teeth, but they also had almost no cavities. This horse-and-buggy dentist set out to find the reason and discovered that there was an abnormal amount of natural fluoride in the water of that area. A careful researcher, he administered water with less fluoride; the stain disappeared, but the teeth still resisted decay. McCay had discovered fluoride's cavity-prevention characteristics, easing the agony of millions of people throughout the world!

Born at Lawrence, Massachusetts, in 1874, McKay graduated from the University of Pennsylvania Dental School in 1900 and set up practice in Colorado Springs the next year. It was in 1908 that he first noticed the effects of the fluoride.

He was the recipient of many national awards, including the highest honor of the American Dental Association. His research ultimately led to the fluoridation of water systems and fluoride additives to tooth cleansers,

McKay left Colorado Springs and did research at other laboratories several times during his career but settled permanently there in 1940. He died in 1959 at the age of 85.

Her Statue Stands in the National Capitol . . .

Florence Rena Sabin

Once, when asked about the most exciting moment in her life, Florence Sabin replied that it was the night she "witnessed the birth of the first blood vessels in the embryo of a chicken and had seen the first beat of a heart." This from a woman who had, among other notable experiences, dined with the great Albert Einstein. Florence Sabin was the first woman professor at Johns Hopkins University and the first woman to be elected to life membership in the National Academy of Science.

Born in Central City in 1871, her mother died when Sabin was only seven years old, so she and her sister, Mary, were sent to New England. She graduated from Vermont Academy and went on to a degree in zoology at Smith College. After teaching for a year at Wolfe Hall in Denver, she was admitted to Johns Hopkins, where she attained her MD and was retained on the faculty.

Her experimental work with lymphatic vessels, which drain fluid from the tissues of the body, was only one of her contributions to medicine, winning for her a national prize. She constructed a model of the brain which was used by students throughout the medical world, and her *Atlas of the Medula and Midbrain* became a classic textbook. She wrote hundreds of professional articles.

Sabin also served on several important foundation boards for the furtherance of medical research. In 1925, she went to New York City to become a staff member of the Rockefeller Institute for Medical Research. In 1938, at the age of 67, she retired and moved back to Denver.

Florence Sabin was not a retiring person, though. She continued her work with foundations during World War II and became a noted writer on the philosophy of medicine. Her foundations of life were "honesty, good will, and reasoned optimism." At the end of the war, Governor John Vivian established a committee to look into the health of Colorado and appointed Sabin to lead it. In exhaustive research, she found that one reason Colorado had a higher than average death rate was the lamentable lack of sanitation and public health programs. Her "Sabin Health Bills" passed the state legislature with much difficulty, but the Colorado Health Department finally was able to establish adequate facilities for public health through her efforts, which spanned the terms of four governors.

Florence Sabin retired again in 1951 at the age of eighty. She died in 1953 while standing up to take a seventh inning stretch during a televised Yankees-Dodgers game. In 1958 her native state placed her statue in the nation's capital, the first Coloradan to receive the honor.

Pioneer of Liver Transplants . . .

Thomas Earl Starzl

One of the most famous transplant surgeons in the world did some of his most important research and pioneer surgery at the University of Colorado Medical Center between 1962 and 1980.

Thomas Starzl was born at Le Mares, Iowa, in 1926. He was educated there and at Westminster College (BA) and Northwestern University (MA and MD). He served as an assistant professor at Northwestern and then became a member of the medical faculty.

Starzl married Barbara Brothers in 1954, and they had three children. He moved to Denver in 1962 to become head of the surgical program at the Denver hospital, where he performed early kidney transplants and pioneered in the field of liver transplants. He was also on the research staffs of the University of Miami School of Medicine and the Johns Hopkins Medical School.

In 1964, he published *Experience in Renal Transplantation* and, in 1969, *Experience in Hepatic Transplantation*.

Thomas Starzl left the Denver institution in 1980 to join the University of Pittsburgh where in 1983 he performed the nation's first multiple abdominal organ transplant.

Many honors have come his way, including the Lund University and Malmo [Sweden] Surgical Society award, the Most Outstanding Contribution to Surgical Science Award of the *Prix de la Societe International de Churgie*, the Distinguished Achievement Award for Modern Medicine, the Eppinger Prize for Contribution to Liver Disease Research, and honorary doctorates at the New York Medical College and the University of Wyoming.

Warrior Against the "Dread Destroyer"...

Gerald Bertram Webb

In the latter part of the nineteenth century, tuberculosis (called at that time "philisis") was the world's number one killer. In 1894, Gerald Webb, a 22-year-old British medical student, brought his bride Jennie to Colorado Springs in hopes that the high altitude would cure her of the life-threatening infection. Little was known of the causes and cures of the disease. He completed his medical studies at the University of Denver and established a practice in Manitou Springs. Immediately he went to work to establish the reason lymphocytes, the white cells that combat disease, are more numerous in the body at higher altitudes.

Jennie died of tuberculosis in 1903. The next year, Gerald married the granddaughter of Confederacy President Jefferson Davis, and they journeyed to London to study with the eminent bacteriologist Sir Almont Wright, concentrating on immunity. The marriage produced two sons. During World War I, Webb, now a naturalized American citizen, served as a medical officer in France. On his return, he founded the American Association of Immunologists and later became the youngest president of the National Tuberculosis Association. He became president of the Association of American Physicians and won the Trudeau Medal for his research on immunology.

His second wife, Varina, died in 1934 of blood poisoning resulting from a scratch from a hatpin. Despondent, Gerald plunged even deeper into his research, writing two books on tuberculosis, plus biographical studies. He became a medical professor with the University of Colorado, where the Webb-Waring Medical Building was named for him and his successor in the research. His initial research led to many other discoveries which helped fight the "dread destroyer."

Among his adventures in Colorado was his service as the physician to Theodore Roosevelt on his famous hunting trip near Silt.

Among those who visited him in Colorado Springs and Denver were novelist Thomas Mann and poet Carl Sandburg. He was an adviser to another famous doctor, **Florence Sabin**. Webb died in 1948.

The Scientists

Nobelist of Genetic Engineering ...
Thomas Cech

Elucidating on how RNA, a basic genetic material, can both carry information and act as a catalyst within living cells won a 1989 Nobel Prize for Thomas Cech of the University of Colorado. (He shared the honors with Sidney Altman of Yale, a C.U. alumnus.)

Cech was born in Chicago in 1948 and reared in the Champaign-Urbana area of Illinois and at Iowa City, Iowa. He was an undergraduate at Grinnell College and went on to a doctorate in chemistry at the University of California, Berkeley, in 1975. After that, the scholar continued post-doctoral work at Massachusetts Institute of Technology before accepting a faculty position at the University of Colorado in 1978. Five years later, he was Professor of Biochemistry and Molecular Biology.

National attention came in 1982, when he published the revolutionary paper, "Self-splicing RNA: Autoercision and Autocyclization of the Ribosomal RNA Intervening Sequence of Tetrahymena" in *Cell Magazine.*

Cech met his wife Carol, a biochemist at C.U., early in his career, and they had two daughters when the ultimate honor in science came to him in October of 1989.

Western Slope Farm Boy Who Won the Nobel Prize ...
Willard Frank Libby

The first chemistry lab in which Willard Libby worked was composed of little more than Mason jars and scavenged rubber tubing, but he went on to become a Nobel Prize winner. He discovered the "atomic time clock," more popularly known as the Carbon-14 system, for dating artifacts up to 50,000 years old. The world's archaeological community depends more upon this system than any other for dating materials of organic origin.

A native of the little town of Grand Valley (now known as Parachute), Libby was the son of industrious farm parents. He was born in 1908 and reared on the farm. After high school in Grand Valley, he went to the University of California, where he earned his BS and PhD and served on the faculty as a professor of physics and astrophysics. He became the father of twin daughters in 1949.

At the University of Chicago and the University of California at Los Angeles, he worked out the concept that deteriorating organic matter gives off radioactive waves, the amount of which can determine the age of the material. It won him the Albert Einstein Award in 1959 and, in 1960, one of the world's most prestigious honors, the Nobel Prize for Chemistry. His famous book, *Radiocarbon Dating*, was published four years previously, but it took an astonished scientific world some time to test further and accept the validity of his famous contribution.

In his later career, he worked on chemistry as related to the space program and on tritium and its use in hydrology and geophysics. He served twice on the Atomic Energy Commission and was a leader in the "Atoms for Peace" program.

Willard Libby retired in 1976 and died in 1980. He received many honorary degrees and awards in addition to the Nobel Prize. In 1988, Sweden issued a postage stamp commemorating him and his achievement.

Energy for Future Generations . . .

Amory Bloch Lovins

World-class energy consultants Amory Lovins and his wife Hunter are the chief figures at the Rocky Mountain

Institute, located at Old Snowmass. From there they advise governments all over the world on new forms of energy use, better utilization of existing energy, and the importance of environmental conservation. Their own home is a showpiece to visitors from throughout the world, 4000 square feet, solar heated, using only a tenth of the electrical energy and a third of the water consumed in similar structures, with no loss in living luxury.

Born in Washington, D.C., in 1947, Lovins attended Harvard and then went to Oxford University for an MA. He became a don at that famous academic bastion at the age of 21, the youngest employed there in four centuries. A policy adviser to the Friends of the Earth in San Francisco from 1971 to 1984, Lovins is the recipient of at least five honorary doctorates, and was a lecturer at the University of California. He founded the Rocky Mountain Institute, which quickly became the nation's most important source of information on the sustainable use of resources. He has been awarded numerous prizes and recognitions for his insightful studies of world conservation.

Among his books, some written with Hunter, are *The Stockholm Conference: Only One Earth, World Energy Strategies, Soft Energy Paths, Non-Nuclear Futures, Breaking the Nuclear Link, Brittle Power,* and *Energy Unbound.* He has written hundreds of articles.

Amory Lovins is also a poet and is much in demand as a speaker and university lecturer.

Solar Astronomer Helped Feed the World . . .

Walter Orr Roberts

There is a popular story that, during World War II, the long-awaited D-Day invasion of the Normandy Coast was fortunately delayed by a message from Climax, Colorado, predicting (correctly) that the weather would be unfavorable on the planned date. Whether true or not, the solar chronograph there, first in the Western Hemisphere, led to many discoveries of the relationship between sun spot activity and weather conditions here on earth. The man who assembled and operated it was Walter Orr Roberts, Harvard and University of Colorado astronomer who went on to make great advances in the science of forecasting, drought prediction, and the effects of climate on world food production.

The director of the High Altitude Observatory in Boulder and Climax, Roberts was a world-wide leader in the field of solar-terrestrial relationships. Born in West Bridgewater, Massachusetts, in 1915, he studied at Amherst College and went on to Harvard, where, in 1943, he was awarded the PhD degree in astrophysics. Roberts led the Solar Research Program and served on the faculties of Harvard, Radcliffe, and the University of Colorado. He was the first astronomer to detect and measure solar spicules, flares which jump out 6,000 miles from the surface of the sun. These flares have the effect of creating changes in weather conditions on earth and disrupting communications.

A visionary in many areas, Walt Roberts raised early warnings about the dangers of global warming, acid rain, and urban smog.

Roberts was awarded the coveted Hodgkins Medal of the Smithsonian Institute, as well as many other prestigious citations. He was associate editor of the *Journal of Geophysical Research* and president of the University Committee on Solar-Terrestrial Relationships. More recently, he has written *Food and Climate Review* for the *Food and Climate Forum*, published by the Aspen Institute. His leadership led to the establishment of the National Center for Atmospheric Research in Boulder and made the University of Colorado a leader in the field of astrophysics.

Ranked as one of America's most distinguished scientists, Roberts died in Boulder in 1990.

The Grand Dame of Anthropology . . .
Ruth Underhill

She lived just a week short of a century, and she spent her lifetime enlightening the world, especially about the *Red Men's America*, the title of one of her 26 books on Native Americans.

Ruth Underhill was born in 1884 at Ossining, New York, and was able to travel to Europe as a teenager. She returned to study at Vassar College and then crossed the Atlantic again to the London School of Economics. Back home in Ossining, she became a teacher of Latin at a boys' military academy, but her fascination with strange tongues led her back to Europe, where she became proficient in four languages and served with the Red Cross following World War I. Her curiosity led her to study at Columbia University in the fields of philosophy, psychology, economics, sociology, and anthropology. Anthropology excited her the most.

Underhill was awarded a fellowship to study the Papago Indians of Arizona, and she moved outdoors, living in an old army tent, and sometimes in caves, to gain the confidence of those gentle natives. She wrote down their songs and poems, and in 1936 she published the *Autobiography of a Papago Woman*, about Chona, a Papago octogenarian. This was followed by other books on the Papagos, the Piutes, and the early Anasazi Indians. She became Professor Underhill at the University of Denver and lived in a simple log home in south Denver.

Retiring from active teaching in 1952, she continued to write about the earliest natives of the West and produced a television documentary in 1959. At the age of 97, she went back into the Indian country of Arizona to help the Mohaves write their history.

Ruth Underhill died in August, 1984, just a week before she would have celebrated her one hundredth birthday.

Digging Up the Really "Old West" ...

H.M. Worthington

Using the Carbon-14 tests developed by Colorado Nobelist **Willard Libby**, Hannah Marie Worthington has conclusively dated the campsites of roving hunters in North America at 9,000 B.C. and maybe even 12,000 B.C. She thinks they may have crossed the Bering Straits far earlier than previously surmised.

Worthington was born in Denver in 1914 and graduated from East High School. She first became interested in archeology while she was a student at the University of Colorado. After graduation in 1935 she joined the staff of the Denver Museum of National History and became Curator of Archeology in 1937, whereupon she led the first museum expedition in its history, working in Montrose County to excavate two primitive rock shelters. In 1940, she married petroleum geologist George Volk, while continuing her studies which led to an MA and PhD degree from Radcliffe College, in cooperation with Harvard University.

Her *Ancient Man in North America* (1939) sold a record number of copies for a scholarly work and established her as an international authority on the topic, leading to speeches in Europe and Africa. She was the first Coloradan to receive the Guggenheim Award for scientific achievement. Her field studies were high adventure, including an incident in which she rescued a co-worker with a burst appendix, driving 75 miles over primitive trails to a Grand Junction hospital.

Among her other works are *Prehistoric Man in the Southwest* and *Ancient Hunters and Gatherers of America*. She left the Denver Museum in 1968 and has continued to work with museums at the University of Colorado and Colorado College, as well as serving as visiting professor at Arizona State University. Her special forte is Folsom Man.

The Naturalists

Natural Philosopher From the Plains . . .

Harold "Hal" Borland

Though he was born in Nebraska in 1900, Hal Borland spent most of his formative years in Flagler, as related in his autobiographical *Country Editor's Boy*. As a member of the Naval Reserve in World War I, he was still too young to go to sea. He returned to help his father edit the *Flagler News* before becoming a reporter for the *Denver Post*. After that, he wandered all over the nation, reporting for newspapers and syndicated associations in New York, Brooklyn, Salt Lake City, Fresno, San Diego, Ashville, North Carolina, and Marshall, Texas. During a stint back in his beloved plains country, he edited the *Stratton Press* for a year, but then returned to national posts in Philadelphia and for the *New York Times Magazine*, where he served as a regular columnist for the rest of his life.

His range of talent in writing was enormous. Although he was most famous for his works on naturalist topics, he preferred to be called a "natural philosopher," and indeed his columns were read throughout the world for the wisdom as well as the nature items. Hal Borland published three volumes of poetry, wrote radio scripts, documentary films, movies, and novels. As outdoor editor of the Sunday *Times*, he wrote the *History of Wildlife in America*.

As a novelist, Borland wrote for both children and adults. *Valor, the Story of a Dog* was his most popular juvenile novel, while his most honored novel was *When The Legends Die*, a story of a Ute boy from Pagosa Springs who joined the rodeo circuit. It was published in nine languages and was made into a movie. His *High, Wide and Lonesome* was another autobiography. He wrote some of his material under the pseudonym of "Ward West."

During his later years, Hal moved with his wife to Sharon, Connecticut, where he continued his prolific writing career, often coming back to the Colorado prairies. Hal Borland died in 1978 at Sharon.

Founder of National Forest Wilderness Areas . . .

Arthur Hawthorne Carhart

Referred to as the "dean of U.S. conservationists," Arthur Carhart was the first landscape architect employed by the United States Forest Service and creator of the concept that certain areas of the forest should be preserved in their pristine state, closed to motor traffic and all economic development.

Carhart was born in 1892 in Mapleton, Iowa, and earned an MS degree at Iowa State College. During World War I he served as lieutenant in the U.S. Army, and then joined the Forest Service as a ranger, assigned to the Trapper's Lake region of White River National Forest in Colorado. It was there that he first experimented with the idea of a wilderness area, and its success led to the establishment of the Quetico-Superior Wilderness Area in Minnesota, the first officially designated wilderness area. (Aldo Leopold, usually given credit for the idea, acknowledged that Carhart was the originator.)

Carhart left the Forest Service to become a city planner but was more noted for his conservation writing. He wrote 24 books and hundreds of articles, mostly on conservation, and received numerous awards for distinguished service to conservation. He settled in Denver, where he served as executive secretary of the Denver Planning Commission. He established the Conservation Library of North America at the Denver Public Library. In 1956, Carhart won the Izaak Walton League's Founder's Award.

He wrote short stories and wildlife stories for all ages, as well as guides to fishing treatises on forestry and water, and even a volume on Colorado history. His wife, Vera, died in

1966, and soon after that he moved to Escondido, California, where he died in 1978.

America's First National Forest Ranger . . .

William R. Kreutzer

A strapping young man of 20 years, Bill Kreutzer rode his horse into Denver from Sedalia and applied for a job as a forest ranger with the Forest Reserve system. Even though reserves had been set aside in 1891, the laws concerning grazing, mining, and lumbering had never been enforced, and now it was rumored that the federal government was going to hire a ranger for the Plum Creek reserve near Bill's home. After some complications over his youth and politics, Bill, the son and grandson of foresters trained in Germany, was given the appointment, becoming the first forest ranger in the nation.

Most folks didn't want the government to restrict the use of forest lands in those days, and in his early career he was the target of gunshots more than once. Bill fought forest fires alone and was burned many times. Political pressure led to his transfer to Battlement Mesa Reserve, with authority at Collbran, and then Cedaredge when the region was changed to Grand Mesa National Forest. Bill had to persuade unwilling ranchers to rotate their grazing lands, serve as a go-between in disputes between cattle and sheep ranchers, try to stop random clear-cutting of timber, and even restrict mining operations. He was on the front line of the battle for preservation and multiple use as opposed to the "Git and Grab" philosophy of Colorado's early settlers.

His friendly manner, his cowboy background, and his high principles gradually won him acceptance by ranchers, foresters, and miners and a promotion to supervisor of the Gunnison National Forest. Bill fell in love and married at Gunnison. In 1921, he was appointed supervisor of Colorado National Forest, surrounding Rocky Mountain National Park, and spent the rest of his career headquartered at Fort Collins.

When he retired in 1939, he had served longer than any man in the history of the service—41 years.

Very few Coloradans have mountains named for them, but Mount Kreutzer, near Tincup in Gunnison County, was named for Bill, who died in 1956 at Fort Collins.

Father of Rocky Mountain National Park . . .

Enos A. Mills

Like many other people who became famous in Colorado, Enos Mills came to the high altitude for health reasons. Born in Fort Scott, Kansas, in 1870, he suffered from lung disease so his family moved to Estes Park when he was fourteen years old. As his constitution improved, he was able to take work in hotels there, and then became a cowboy. He served as a guide for several survey parties studying the famous peaks west of the village.

It was then that he became infatuated with the beauty of the mountains and began writing about them. His articles on the mountains appeared in such magazines as the *Saturday Evening Post, McClure's,* and *Sunset.*

At the age of twenty, Mills built a cabin at the foot of Longs Peak and later opened the Longs Peak Inn, ten miles west of Estes Park.

In 1909, Mills began a campaign to turn 600 square miles of the region into a national park, and James Grafton Rogers, a Denver political leader, drafted the legislation. It took many books and articles to convince Congress, but in 1915 Rocky Mountain National Park was finally established, with an area of 400 square miles.

Mills was a naturalist of nationwide fame, writing *The Spell of the Rockies, Wild Life in the Rockies, Bird Memories of the Rockies, Adventures of a Nature Guide,* and *Your National Parks.*

He is believed to be the first person to ascend Longs Peak in the winter. Mills had many other exciting adventures in the park, including survival while snowbound at timberline. Among his other contributions, he established wildlife conferences at the park.

Enos Mills died in 1922.

The Music Makers

World-Renowned Symphony Conductor . . .

Antonia Brico

"Stokowski once got real sarcastic with me; he seemed to think I should stay home!" That was a comment from Antonia Brico, who became probably the greatest woman conductor in the world after spending the better part of her lifetime bucking prejudice against women in her chosen career.

Born in Holland in 1902, her family moved to San Francisco just after the earthquake of 1906. At the age of 17, she attended the University of California and studied under the great Paul Steindorf. When she confided her ambition to direct orchestras, he warned her, "You'll never make it," but he hadn't reckoned on what she called her "Dutch stubbornness." She then studied in Berlin and Milan and conducted her first orchestra at Genoa, Italy. She then founded the Women's Orchestra of New York. Her friends included composer Jan Sibelius, Artur Rubenstein, Bruno Walter, Wilhelm Furtwaengler, and the famous doctor-philosopher Albert Schweitzer, whom she visited in Africa and Germany six times. In 1927, she became the first American ever admitted to the Berlin State Academy of Music.

She moved to Denver in 1942 to direct the Civic Orchestra, and in 1947 founded the Denver Businessmen's Orchestra, which later came to be known as the Brico Symphony. Antonia was in demand as a guest conductor in London, at the Hollywood Bowl, New York's Lincoln Center, and with the National Symphony in Washington, D.C., as well as in Manila, Seattle, Nova Scotia, and Carnegie Hall. After she had established her reputation, she was invited to conduct the Denver Symphony Orchestra. In addition, she served some time as a professor of music at Colorado College, Colorado Springs.

One of her students from Denver, **Judy Collins**, produced an award-winning documentary about her in 1974:

Antonia, A Portrait of a Woman. She continued her world-wide tours, finally laying down the baton in 1984, when her orchestra was renamed the Centennial Philharmonic. She was married only to her art.

Gold Platter Folk Singer . . .
Judy Collins

Born in Seattle in 1939, Judy Collins came to Denver as a teenager and studied with symphony conductor **Antonia Brico**, about whom she later produced an award-winning documentary film. Judy's fame was built mainly on folk music and songs of political protest during the Vietnam War. She made her first public appearance in Boulder in 1959.

Her career then took off, sending her to major concert halls in the United States and Europe. She made at least six gold L-P recordings. She also made other movies, working both as an actress and producer. Her autobiography, *Trust Your Heart*, is a touching account of her generation's struggle during the trying days of the Sixties.

Popular Singer Who Became an Environmentalist . . .
John Denver (Henry John Deutschendorf, Jr.)

As a singer, composer, and actor, John Denver won America's heart. He continued his singing career while developing the Windstar Institute at Snowmass, seeking better ways of living in harmony with nature and with other people on this planet.

Born in 1943 at Roswell, New Mexico, he was inspired by the songs of Elvis Presley and studied guitar. Deutschendorf majored in architecture at Texas Tech in Lubbock but dropped out to take to the concert stage as a folk singer. It was in Southern California that he changed his name to John Denver, playing with the Chad Mitchell Trio. Among his most famous compositions were "Leaving on a Jet Plane," "Follow Me," and "Back Home Again." He appeared in a number of movies, starring with George Burns in *Oh, God!* and in a remake of *Mr. Smith Goes to Washington.*

In the Bicentennial American Music Awards, Denver was voted Best Male Vocalist in Pop-Rock and also Best Male Vocalist in Country Music for his album *Back Home Again.*

He moved to Aspen, establishing his noted Windstar Institute at Snowmass to promote environmental harmony. His career in musical harmony continues.

World-Class Violinist . . .

Eugene Fodor

In 1974, Russian judges couldn't decide among three contestants—the young American, Eugene Fodor, and two Russian violinists, so they awarded them all second place. This made Fodor the first American to win the prestigious Tschaikovsky Competition and assured a stellar role in the music world to a boy born on North Turkey Creek near Morrison in 1950 and educated in the Golden schools.

His father, a Morrison excavation contractor and garage operator, was a dedicated amateur violinist, and when Eugene was eight he was allowed to study with Harold Wippler, concertmaster of the Denver Symphony Orchestra. At eleven, he won his first competition at the Kiwanis Club's national youth camp for musicians. Then came victory in the Merriweather Post competition. In 1972, he won the coveted Niccolo Paganini Competition in Genoa, Italy, and later appeared in New York's Avery Fisher Hall.

High school took him to New York City, where he received a full scholarship to the Juilliard School, and then he moved on to the University of Southern California where he studied with the famous Jascha Heifitz. He finished his formal education at Indiana University, Bloomington. Fodor also studied with such masters of the violin as Joseph Gingold, Mischa Mischakoff, and Ivan Galamian.

In 1977, he bought a ranch adjoining his father's property near Morrison, where he could take vacations from the concert stage and enjoy horseback riding. He is also a jogger and scuba diver.

Writer, Singer, and Mayor of Ouray . . .
C.W. McCall (Bill Fries)

A commercial for Old Home Bread led C.W. McCall into a singing and composing career as a pop star, even though his own preference is for classical music.

Born Bill Fries in 1929 in Iowa, he still uses the name of Fries, with the C.W. McCall name reserved strictly for his songs. The "C.W." stands for country western, and he liked the title of *McCall's* magazine.

Fries was an Omaha advertising man when he decided the best way to promote his bread client was with an original song, "Old Home Filler-up and Keep On Truckin' Cafe in Pisgah, Iowa." This led to many other popular tunes, the most famous of which was "Convoy," dear to truckers everywhere.

Among the hits which promoted Colorado was "Wolf Creek Pass." Soon his albums were hitting the best-seller lists.

Fries regularly vacationed in Ouray and finally moved there permanently. With his family he worked out a magnificent multi-media presentation which is shown nightly in the summer to capacity crowds. Based on the splendor of the San Juan Mountains, it is accompanied by recorded music of the London Symphony.

He was elected mayor of Ouray.

The Man with the Greatest Swing Band ...

Glenn Miller

To this day, Glenn Miller's famous band recordings are among the best sellers for those who love the era of "Big Band" swing. His brief career is remembered as the epitome of the music style so popular at the outset of World War II.

Glenn Miller was born in 1904 at Clarinda, Iowa. His family moved to Fort Morgan when he was still a boy, and it was there that he graduated from high school, already playing the trombone in local dance band groups. After graduation, he joined the Boyd Senter Band, traveling the West. It wasn't until he was twenty that he decided to enroll at the University of Colorado, where he played with Holly Moyer's local ensemble for a year before dropping out to travel with several other orchestras, both as an arranger and trombonist. He married Colorado University co-ed Helen Burger in 1928 while with Ben Pollach's orchestra. He was also doing a number of stints in the pits of Broadway musicals at the time.

It was his arranging ability that earned him an invitation to join the Dorsey Brothers' band, already nationally famous in 1934, and he did their arrangements of "Peg O' My Heart" and "On Moonlight Bay." Three years later, Miller formed his own band and broadcast from such ballrooms as the Roosevelt Hotel in New Orleans and the Raymore in Boston. Because of internal discord and personal misfortunes, he disbanded the group, starting another in 1938.

For his new orchestra, he composed his famous theme song, "Moonlight Serenade," and made popular such hits as "In the Mood," "Tuxedo Junction," and "Chattanooga Choo-Choo."

Miller volunteered for the Army in 1942, following the attack on Pearl Harbor, and developed an All-Service, All-Star Band to entertain the troops. He was flying from England to Paris on December 14, 1944, when his single engine plane disappeared, and no trace of it was ever found. That was the year when every fifth piece played on jukeboxes was a Glenn Miller performance.

Hollywood later filmed a story of his life, starring James Stewart as Glenn and June Allyson as Helen.

Famed Black Jazz Musician of the Roaring Twenties . . .

George Morrison

From Boulder to a command performance before the king and queen of England, playing a violin and leading one of the nation's great all-black orchestras, George Morrison overcame racial prejudice to take a major role in the introduction of jazz to the world. He was born in poverty in Fayette, Missouri, one of fourteen children whose parents were locally noted as musicians. They moved to Boulder in 1900 when George was nine years old and already performing on the violin. Soon after, the family group started playing the mining camps as the Morrison Brothers String Band.

Morrison married Willa May, and they moved to Denver. He had worked at odd jobs to take advanced music lessons and dreamed of playing with the Denver Symphony, but racial attitudes made such a career unthinkable in those days. He did lead a band that played wherever it could; in many places he could not have attended as a customer because of his race. Beginning in parlor houses, including that of the famed Mattie Silks, he later led an eleven-piece band at the Albany Hotel and for many years played for the *Denver Post* special train to the Cheyenne Frontier Days.

The Morrisons had two children. The family left Denver for a time to study classical music in Chicago, playing early jazz there. Then he formed his own jazz band and began to tour the nation. His fame led to New York, where he became a recording artist for Columbia Records, and then to a tour of Europe in 1920 where he played a command performance for King George and Queen Mary of England. After his return, he was among the most popular band leaders in the nation. He returned to Denver where he opened a night club, but was forced to give up in the unhappy Ku Klux Klan revival of

1925. However, for several decades after that time, Morrison and his orchestra played for Colorado and continued to maintain a national image. One of his further contributions to music history was the introduction of **Paul Whiteman** to New York record studios, and the introduction to show business of **Hattie McDaniel**, who sang with his band on tour before her later fame as an Academy Award winner in *Gone With the Wind*.

George Morrison died in Denver in 1974.

The King of Jazz . . .

Paul Whiteman

A young Denverite was playing with the People's Symphony in San Francisco when he dropped into a Barbary Coast dive and heard jazz. He found it "raucous," "crude," and "unmusical," but rhythmic and "as catching as small-pox and spirit-lifting." From that time on, Paul Whiteman could not stay with strictly classical music, but began a career blending the cold jazz into mellow refinement and gaining the title "King of Jazz" by 1930.

Paul Whiteman was born in Denver in 1890, son of Denver's noted public school music director, Wilberforce Whiteman. He studied violin at an early age and played with **Gene Fowler**, greasing streetcar tracks and eventually landing in Judge **Ben Lindsey**'s juvenile court. He was enrolled in several Denver high schools and spent a short time at the University of Denver before going to San Francisco. His career there was interrupted by World War I. He joined the Navy and formed an orchestra with sailors at Bear Island, California. After the Armistice, Whiteman formed a new jazz group which was an instant success, playing some of the most prestigious ballrooms in America.

Among early hits were "The Japanese Sandman," which had sales of over two million records, and "Three O'Clock in the Morning." While the phonograph business was booming, radio was to become ever more popular, and Whiteman's band was one of the first to be nationally broadcast. On the New York stage, his was the star act in George White's Follies.

Probably the preeminent example of the merging of jazz and classics was Whiteman's premier performance of Gershwin's "Rhapsody in Blue" in 1924. His rendition of "Whispering" was an all-time best-seller. Whiteman also introduced Deems Taylor's "Circus Days" and Ferde Grofe's "Grand Canyon Suite."

In his later years, the "King of Jazz" founded the Whiteman Awards, based on an annual "symphonic jazz" competition. He was made music director for the Blue Network of NBC (which later became ABC).

During his career, he performed many times in Europe and finally returned to Denver, where his orchestra packed the Red Rocks Amphitheater. He spent his final years on a ranch in Colorado where he could enjoy the mountains once more. Whiteman died in 1967.

The Entertainers

Rope-Walker and Balloonist . . .
Ivy Baldwin (Willie Ivy)

One of the world's most renowned aerial performers made his headquarters in Denver during the height of his career. The man just could not resist walking both tight and loose ropes across deep canyons or making parachute jumps from balloons before the era of aviation. He performed his stunts throughout the United States, Java, Mexico, Borneo, and Europe.

Willie Ivy was born in San Antonio, Texas, in 1866 and moved to Denver as a youngster. For a while, he performed with a troupe known as the Baldwin Brothers and adopted the name by which he became famous: Ivy Baldwin.

Baldwin joined the Signal Corps during the Spanish-American War and survived when his observation balloon was shot down. He contracted with Elitch Gardens, a Denver amusement park, to perform regularly, and made it his international headquarters.

He was the second man in the nation to make a parachute jump. (The first was his touring partner, Tom Baldwin.) His most spectacular feats, though, were probably his walks across Eldorado Canyon, 582 feet above the streambed, first on a tight rope and later on a loose rope swaying in the wind.

Dropping from high above city streets in Chicago and New York, he showed many urban dwellers their first sight of a parachute jump. Baldwin was among the first inductees to the Colorado Aviation Hall of Fame.

Late in life, he made his home at Marshdale, near Evergreen. At the age of 82, he took another walk across the canyon at Eldorado Springs; his eighty-sixth stroll across the ravine there! If he ever came close to falling, he never admitted it. He lived to the age of 87, dying in 1953 in Arvada.

Boss of the Wagon Train . . .
Ward Bond

Movie star Ward Bond was born in Denver in 1905 and received his first taste of acting in the schools there before moving to Los Angeles to study dramatics at the University of Southern California.

Bond entered the movie industry after graduation and from 1929 until 1959 had supporting roles in more than 200 films. He was chosen, along with John Wayne, to star in *Salute*, a John Ford film, beginning a lifetime friendship of the three movie personalities.

He was star of the television series *Wagon Train*, as the boss of the operation, until his death in 1960. His last home was Dallas, Texas.

Bubbling Movie Actress . . .
Spring Byington

Spring Byington was a support actress most noted for her effervescent personalities. Her sparkling style won her an Academy Award nomination for her role in *You Can't Take it With You* in 1938. Not only did she appear in more than ninety films, but she starred on television's *December Bride* series and appeared in several episodes of *Laramie*.

Born in 1893 at Colorado Springs, she attended the schools there before setting out on a dramatic career which took her to stock theaters and Broadway before her screen debut as Marmee, the mother in *Little Women*, filmed in 1933.

Among other films in her four-decade career were *Roxie Hat, Heaven Can Wait, In the Good Old Summer Time,* and *Please Don't Eat the Daisies*. Spring Byington died in 1971.

Horrifier of the Silent Movies . . .
Alonzo "Lon" Chaney

As the *Hunchback of Notre Dame* and the *Phantom of the Opera*, Lon Chaney was perhaps the actor who brought the horror movie into its own, way back in the days before sound.

He was born in Colorado Springs in 1883 and at twelve was already a prop boy and scene painter at a theater there. Six years later he toured with his brother's stock company and then went to California to do song-and-dance routines in a variety show. By 1912, Lon Chaney was doing slapstick for the silent movies; it was then that he began experimenting with the macabre and grotesque make-up which brought screams from audiences for more than a decade. He used 72 pounds of rubber to create a hunch for the hunchback and placed wires in his nostrils, making them point upward to resemble the skull of the phantom. The film that made him a star was *The Miracle Man*, in 1919. His only talking film was *The Unholy Three*, produced just before his death in 1930.

Chaney married Cleva Creighton in 1905, and their son, Lon, Jr., continued the tradition of horror film roles his father had established. In his stellar career the elder Chaney appeared in more than 150 films, mostly centered on the bizarre and macabre.

"Truth or Consequences" Led to "This Is Your Life" . . .
Ralph Livingstone Edwards

When he was a young boy in Merino, where he was born in 1913, Ralph Edwards used to play the game "Truth or Consequences" with his family and friends. Although the family moved to Oakland, California, when he was eleven, he never forgot the days in Merino. When his career took him into nationwide radio, he made the show "Truth or

Consequences" so famous that people huddled around the radio and laughed themselves to tears. The town of Hot Springs, New Mexico, was so taken with the show that it changed its name to Truth or Consequences.

His success with that show continued on into the years of television, when he added another famous and popular show, "This is Your Life," in which a celebrity was given a surprise re-enactment of his or her career and then met family and friends who had secretly come to take part in the show.

Both productions made television history. His later career has included widespread speeches and performances for worthy causes.

Swashbuckler of the Early Flicks . . .
Douglas Fairbanks

There is a story that when he was a student at West High School in Denver, Douglas Fairbanks, bored with a study hall, leaped out of the second-floor window, landed spryly on his feet, and ran to freedom for the day. In any event, he was noted for his agility and acrobatics, and that was one of the talents which made him a movie idol—along with his strikingly handsome face, of course.

He was born Douglas Elton Ulman in Denver in 1883, but his mother re-assumed the name of her first husband, Fairbanks, after divorcing Ulman. He grew up in the company of such boys as **Paul Whiteman** and **Gene Fowler** and after one incident was lectured in the court of **Ben Lindsey**, the famous judge. Douglas attended the Colorado School of Mines at Golden, and was enrolled as a special student at Harvard for a short time. He had begun acting with a Denver theatrical troupe at the age of twelve and had taken part in several stage tours, but his Harvard experience led him to Wall Street in New York. However, the lure of Broadway was too strong, and in 1902 he landed a part in the play, *Her Lord and Mate*. Fairbanks was a success, and by 1913 he had his first starring role in *He Comes Up Smiling*.

Hollywood called him, and he starred in the silent movie *His Picture in the Papers* in 1916. Gradually, he began to appear in flamboyant costumes in adventure movies which emphasized his spectacular talents as a dashing sword-fighter: *The Mark of Zorro, Thief of Baghdad, Robin Hood, Three Musketeers, The Gaucho,* and others. In 1930, he starred with Mary Pickford in Shakespeare's *The Taming of the Shrew.* Fairbanks also founded his own production company in the late 1930s.

He wrote books to inspire others in the art of living, including such titles as *Laugh and Live, Making Life Worth While, My Secret Success,* and *Youth Points the Way.* They sold very well, but one critic suggested that their success was due to the photos of the dashing Fairbanks scattered throughout; he was more successful as an actor.

Married three times, he was the father of Douglas Fairbanks, Jr., who inherited his good looks and athletic skills, although the son lamented that he was "victimized by Father's fame." Fairbanks died in 1939.

Host of the Original Amateur Hour . . .

Ted Mack

One of Colorado's contributions to the world of radio and television, Ted Mack, was born in Greeley in 1904. He later moved to Denver, where he attended Sacred Heart High School and the University of Denver. He married Marguerite Overholt before taking up the life of a big band tour. He played with Ben Polloch's Orchestra for two years, and in 1927 became the emcee of a Los Angeles vaudeville orchestra.

Mack founded his own band the next year and continued to tour America until 1935, when he became musical conductor for Metro Goldwyn Mayer movies in Hollywood. One of the most popular radio shows of the time was Major Bowles' Original Amateur Hour, with its famous "gong" for poor performances. Mack became the chief talent scout for the program in 1935 and continued that role, selecting the best talent in the nation (and a few "gongers") until Bowles had to leave the show due to failing health in 1948. Ted Mack was named to succeed Bowles, and the program entered the new medium of television under his leadership.

Another show Ted Mack re-established was the famous Family Hour on radio and television. He also wrote a volume of quotations and inspirational words for thought. Among his philanthropic endeavors were the Ted Mack Foundation for Young Americans and a co-educational children's camp at Great Barrington, Massachusetts.

Academy Award Winner in *Gone with the Wind* . . .

Hattie McDaniel

The first black ever to win an Academy Award was Hattie McDaniel, who portrayed the beloved role of "Mamie" in one of the most famous motion pictures of all time, *Gone With the Wind*. She won the Oscar for Best Supporting Role for her performance in the 1939 classic.

Born in Wichita, Kansas, in 1895, Hattie McDaniel moved with her family to Denver at an early age and attended the 24th Street Elementary School, graduating from East High School. It was during her high school days that she launched her acting career with a reading before the Denver chapter of the Women's Christian Temperance Union. She later acknowledged that she was mortified with fear, but she received a standing ovation nonetheless.

After graduation, she joined a traveling tent show operated by her brother Otis. In 1924, **George Morrison**'s famous orchestra introduced Hattie as its vocalist in nationwide radio broadcasts. Later, she joined the nightclub circuit, and her rendition of the "Saint Louis Blues" at Sam Peck's suburban inn in Milwaukee started her on a new career which eventually took her to Hollywood. Another of her brothers, Sam "Deacon" McDaniel, was a film actor there, and in 1931 Hattie made her first of more than 300 movies.

Many of the parts she played were not flattering to her race, including humorous servant roles and melodramatic white-men's impressions of black mothers. However, as Scarlett O'Hare's "Mamie" she won the hearts of millions by her sensitive characterization.

McDaniel also starred in the radio series *Beulah* and performed with Will Rogers in *Judge Priest*, Paul Robeson in *Show Boat*, and Shirley Temple in *The Little Corporal*.

Hattie married James Lloyd Crawford in 1941, when she was in her mid-forties. She contracted cancer several years later and died in 1952.

The "Tonys" Were Named in Her Memory . . .

Antoinette Perry

Every year, the legitimate stage of America gives out the famous Tony Award for the year's best play, actors, actresses, writers, and directors. It is the equivalent of the film world's Academy Award. Few people realize that the term "Tony" comes from the name of Antoinette Perry, the Denver-born actress and director in whose memory these awards are presented.

She was born in 1888 and made her first appearances on the stage while a high school student. She made a professional debut in Chicago in 1905. Her talent, discovered by star David Belasco, soon led her to New York City, where she became one of the reigning ladies of the stage. Her major plays, *The Music Master* and *Miss Temple's Telegram*, were hits, but in 1909 she left the theater to become the wife of Frank W. Frueauff, who became general manager of the Denver Gas and Electric Company. They had two daughters, Margaret and Elaine. (Elaine later became a star in her own right.) When Frank died in 1922, Antoinette returned to the stage and, after some more triumphant appearances, decided to become a director. Among her achievements in that role were the Kaufman-Ferber play, *Mincik,* and *Strictly Dishonorable*, which ran 563 performances. She continued with *Personal Appearance, Ceiling Zero, Kiss the Boys Goodbye,* and *Going Home.* She was the director of *Harvey,* by Denver's **Mary Chase,** which won a 1945 Pulitzer Prize. She had earlier directed Chase's *Now You've Done It.*

Perry became president of Experimental Theater, Inc., and chairman of the American Theater Wing, serving during World War II, when she established the famous Stage Door Canteen in New York. During her service, she sent out as many as 1,200 performers per month to entertain American troops.

After her death in 1946 at the age of 58, the American Theater Wing honored her by establishing the Antoinette Perry Award and by reconstructing the Stagedoor Canteen. Frank Fay, who had the stellar role of Elwood in *Harvey,* acted as master of ceremonies in the event, which made the Tony one of the most coveted of all dramatic achievements.

First Radio and Television Newscaster . . .

Lowell Thomas

"Good evening, everybody, this is Lowell Thomas," began the introduction to his numerous radio and television broadcasts. This world traveler and adventurer had a life as exciting as those he chronicled from every continent on earth.

Born in Woodington, Ohio, in 1892, he came to Colorado with his family when they moved to Victor in its boom days of the nineties. They later moved to Cripple Creek and then back to Ohio. He attended Northern Indiana State University for a time, returning to Cripple Creek to report for, and then edit, the local newspaper. At 19, he moved to Denver to attend the University of Denver. Supporting himself through free-lance writing, he graduated in 1913 and earned an MA degree the next year before moving to Chicago.

In 1915, Thomas outfitted and headed expeditions to the Arctic and earned a second MA and a faculty position at

Princeton. In 1917, President Wilson appointed him historian of World War I, and he was attached to the armies of Belgium, France, Italy, Serbia, Britain, Arabia and the United States in his coverage. It was on this duty that he discovered the exploits of the legendary "Lawrence of Arabia" and brought them to the attention of the world.

A post-war speaking tour found him accompanying the Prince of Wales on an exploration in India; he went on to visit unknown regions of Burma, Malaya and Tibet. His wife, Frances Ryan, sometimes accompanied him on his travels. Their son, Lowell, Jr., was born in 1923.

The first round-the-world air flight was recorded by Thomas as a movie travel feature, and this led to a series of travelogues by this energetic wanderer. He also broadcast accounts of far-away places on radio.

In 1930, Thomas had the first regular radio newscast, and he produced the first regular television newscast in 1939. Later, he produced and starred in the TV series, *High Adventure*. During World War II, he continued his radio commentaries, still traveling to where the action was.

His books explored the mysteries of Tibetan Lamaism and took readers into the jungles to find lost temples. They included, in addition to the account of Lawrence of Arabia, the *Seven Wonders of the World, History as You Heard It, The Vital Spark, 101 Outstanding Lives, Book of High Mountains,* and *Raiders of the Deep*.

His wife, Frances, died in 1975 after a marriage of 58 years. Before his own passing in 1981, Thomas wrote his autobiography, entitled *Good Evening, Everybody: From Cripple Creek to Samarkand*.

Thomas was very active in bringing attention to the sport of skiing, especially in Colorado, and is honored in the Colorado Ski Hall of Fame at Vail.

The Story Tellers

Contemplating the "Lilies of the Field" . . .

William E. Barrett

His novels often had a delightful and uplifting religious theme. Most famous among them was *Lilies of the Field*, in which a black transient Protestant man helped a group of immigrant Roman Catholic nuns complete a sanctuary in an isolated region of the West. One reviewer maintained that it was inspired by an unfinished church-like stone building in Unaweep Canyon, between Whitewater and Gateway in Western Colorado. The story became a Broadway musical, *Look to the Lilies*, and then the classic motion picture which landed Sidney Poitier an Academy Award.

Born in New York City in 1900, William Barrett attended Manhattan College and came to the Rockies in 1923 to serve as advertising manager for Westinghouse Industries. In 1929, he became a free-lance writer, turning out many short stories and 22 books during his career. His novel *The Left Hand of God* was filmed in 1955, starring Humphrey Bogart, Lee J. Cobb, and Gene Tierney. Barrett's works reflected his abiding faith (he was Roman Catholic) and his crusade for social justice. Another work, *The Wine and the Music*, became the movie *Pieces of Dreams* in 1970. Another highly-praised work was *A Woman in the House*, published in 1971.

Barrett married Christine Rollman in 1925, and they had two children. She died in 1982, and he lived only four years longer. The lovely special collections room at Colorado Women's College in Denver was named in his honor.

The Creator of "Harvey" . . .
Mary Coyle Chase

A famous play on Broadway, *Harvey* is the hilarious story of a beleaguered man and his imaginary drinking companion, a giant rabbit. It was written by Denver's Mary Coyle Chase and directed by **Antoinette Perry**. Chase won the 1945 Pulitzer Prize for the play, which was later made into a movie starring James Stewart.

Chase was a reporter for the *Rocky Mountain News* before she went into full-time dramatic writing. Born in 1907, she went to West High School and then to the University of Denver and the University of Colorado. Her first play, *Me Third*, was written for the Federal Theater Project in Denver in 1936 but was produced on Broadway as *Now You've Done It*.

She wrote a continuous string of famous plays: *A Slip of a Girl* (1941), *The Next Half Hour* (1945), *Mrs. McThing* (1952), *Bernardine* (1952, later made into a movie), *Lolita* (1954), *Midgie Purvis* (1961), and *Cocktails With Mini* (1973).

Mary also wrote several children's books which were best-sellers, including *Loretta Mason Potts* (1958) and *The Wicked Pigeon Ladies in the Garden* (1968).

This prolific writer died in 1981 at the age of 75.

Colorado's Underwater Sea Explorer . . .
Clive Eric Cussler

Far from the oceans he constantly explores, Clive Cussler is a novelist of unique qualities, producing such best-sellers as *Raise the Titanic!* His National Underwater and Marine Agency has made multiple expeditions in search of sunken ships, but not to cash in on the booty found; it is all donated to museums and universities. But that doesn't stop Cussler from creating great novels based on his wide experience as a scavenger *par excellence*.

Born in Aurora, Illinois, in 1931, he studied at Pasadena College and then went into the advertising business in California, with time out for service as a sergeant in the Air Force during the Korean Conflict. Cussler then settled in Denver, where the television commercials he wrote won several awards, leading him into a full-time writing career. He set out to discover historic shipwrecks, and didn't settle for ships of the sea; he found the dirigible Akron, a Navy airship which crashed in 1933 and, more recently, sought to determine if a locomotive lost in a flood long ago on the Colorado prairie was still hidden beneath the creek bed. It wasn't.

Biggest of Cussler's best-sellers were the Titanic story (he predicted almost exactly when it would be found), *Night Probe*, and *Deep Six*. He also writes television scripts and takes part in the filming of his novels.

Married to Barbara Knight, Cussler lives in Arvada and works out of his office in Golden, turning out a new novel almost every year.

A Scribe of the Old West . . .

Mary Hallock Foote

Mary Hallock was brought up in a protective Victorian family in Milton, New York, where she was born in 1847. She loved to write and took art lessons in New York City, but never expected to roam the continent as a writer and illustrator. Her friends were shocked when she married Arthur DeWent Foote, a mining engineer, and traveled to the boom town of Leadville in 1879 to set up housekeeping. There, as she met some of the nation's greatest scientists and explorers, she began her career by writing and illustrating stories of Leadville, published in such magazines as *Scribner's* and *Harper's*.

Her articles led to a series of novels. She was one of the first writers to decry the exploitation of the West by Eastern interests and their lack of concern for the fate of mining towns: Leadville's cornucopia of wealth made fortunes for the **Guggenheims**, the Carnegies, the **Mays**, and the Rockefellers, but little of it ever returned to the town of its origin.

Her novels about Leadville included *The Led-Horse Claim, John Bodewin's Testimony*, and *The Last Assembly Ball*.

She had a son, Arthur, and two daughters, Elizabeth and Agnes. The family moved to other mining areas, including Idaho and Mexico, and finally, Grass Valley, California, where she continued writing, producing seven additional novels.

In 1932, Arthur and Mary left Grass Valley to spend their declining years with Elizabeth in Hingham, Massachusetts, where he died two years later; Mary lived to the age of 91, dying in 1938. Her colorful and sometimes tragic life has been fictionalized by Wallace Stegner in his popular novel, *Angle of Repose*.

Dashing and Urbane Humorist . . .

Gene Fowler

He was working for the *Denver Post* when the colorful and infamous founders of that publication, Frederick Bonfils and Harry Tamen, directed him to kidnap the body of William F. (Buffalo Bill) Cody for internment on Lookout Mountain. Cody was never a resident of Denver, but had died at the home of a relative there. Both Cody, Wyoming, and North Platte, Nebraska, where Cody had maintained ranches, claimed their sites as his preferred burial ground. Gene Fowler, then a young reporter, pulled off the stunt with magnificent flourish, the funeral parade embellished with circus performers from Cody's famed Wild West Show. Cody and North Platte have never forgiven Denver, and for many years the burial site had to be guarded with care.

A native of Colorado, Fowler was born in Denver, but his childhood home was Idaho Springs and its surrounding regions. As a youth, he moved to Denver and attended East High School with **Paul Whiteman** and **Douglas Fairbanks**. After studying at the University of Colorado, Fowler worked for both the *Denver Post* and *Rocky Mountain News* before moving on to New York. Among his acquaintances at the Denver newspapers were **Damon Runyon** and **H. Allen Smith**. Fowler later wrote *Timberline,* about the rambunctious *Post* and its publishers, and an autobiography of his Colorado days, *A Solo in Tom-Toms.*

In New York, Fowler became a popular writer about theater and its notables, with his friends reading like a *Who's Who* of show business. His biography of John Barrymore, *Good Night, Sweet Prince,* was but one of his widely acclaimed memoirs of the famous.

Fowler was himself such an exciting character that he was subject of biographies by his own son Will and by **H. Allen Smith**. His satirical work *Lady Scatterly's Lovers,* a burlesque of D. H. Lawrence's then-forbidden work *Lady Chatterley's Lover,* was written in 1935 but not published until his son found it among his father's papers after his death in 1960.

Western Writer Who Didn't Like Horses . . .

Frederick Glidden (Luke Short)

He wrote more than half a hundred successful Western adventure novels, but admitted he didn't care much for horses. Fred Glidden, whose name became famous as "Luke Short," came to the West from Kewanee, Illinois, where he was born in 1908. It was a circuitous route, with a succession of newspaper jobs following his journalism studies at the Universities of Illinois and Missouri. He almost starved to death as a Canadian fur-trapper and worked on the archaeological diggings at Inscription Rock in El Morro National Park, New Mexico.

After his New Mexico experiences, he tried ranching in Wyoming, but he and horses didn't agree. He met Florence Elder, a Grand Junction native, at a college dance in Greeley. They moved to New Mexico again, where he began writing and she got a job as a housekeeper to support them both. In the late 1940s, they moved to Aspen, where he continued his career in Western fiction. Many of his stories were run as serials in popular magazines. He adopted the name of Luke Short because he thought his own name "sounded too phoney."

Hollywood liked Luke's works and made some of them into movies, including *Station West, Coroner Creek,* and *Blood on the Moon.* Stricken with cancer, Fred Glidden died in Aspen in 1975 at the age of 67, just after completion of his final Western, *Trouble Country.*

Explorer of the Dark Kingdom of the Mind ...

Joanne Greenberg (Hannah Green)

When her novel *I Never Promised You A Rose Garden* was published in 1964 under the pseudonym of Hannah Green, Joanne Greenberg touched the hearts of readers everywhere. The story of a teen-age girl and her fight with mental illness in an institution, it received plaudits from the famous psychologist, Karl Menninger, as well as praise from reviewers, and it sold millions of copies.

Joanne Greenberg was born in Brooklyn, New York, in 1932, and after schooling there, graduated from American University and the University of London. Married and the mother of two children, she has done most of her professional work from her home in Golden. Greenberg has also served as an adjunct professor of anthropology at the Colorado School of Mines and as a certified medical technician with the Lookout Mountain Fire Department.

Among her other works are *The King's Persons, The Monday Voices, In This Sign, Rites of Passage,* and

Summering, a collection of her short stories. *I Never Promised You A Rose Garden* was made into a movie in 1977.

She Spoke Out for the Native Americans . . .

Helen Hunt Jackson

More than a century ago, the U.S. Government was forced to blush and reevaluate its policies when Helen Hunt Jackson published her vituperative *A Century of Dishonor*, condemning the Indian Service for its neglect and persecution of the Native Americans. It was an unpopular position, even in her own Colorado, but it led to an investigation and some improvement in conditions on the reservations.

Mrs. Jackson was an established author, one of the most prolific woman writers of the nineteenth century. A native of Amherst, Massachusetts, she was born in 1830 and orphaned at an early age. She married Edward Hunt in 1852 and was mother of two children, both of whom died in childhood. Hunt, a career army officer, suffocated while experimenting with a "sea-miner" for launching underwater torpedoes during the Civil War. Lonely and desperate, suffering from diphtheria and dyspepsia, Helen moved to Colorado Springs for her health in 1873. There she met the second love of her life, William Sharpless Jackson, whom she wed in 1875.

Helen Hunt Jackson continued to write, and her Eastern friends called to her attention the plight of the Indians. She attacked the Denver establishment over their outrageous defense of the infamous Sand Creek Massacre of Cheyennes a decade earlier, incurring the wrath of such leaders as William Byers, editor of the *Rocky Mountain News*. Finally she wrote her famous non-fiction book indicting the entire government. As a result, she was sent by Secretary of Interior **William Teller** to California to study the Mission Indians. That led to her most famous novel, *Ramona*, still enacted every year in California as a play. When she died of cancer in 1885, her grave in Cheyenne Canyon became such a tourist attraction that the body had to be removed to a cemetery in town.

One of America's Most Famous Novelists . . .

James Albert Michener

He won the Pulitzer Prize for *Tales of the South Pacific* and helped rewrite it into one of Broadway's greatest musical shows. James Michener served on the faculty of what is now the University of Northern Colorado from 1936 to 1942, where he wrote his first successful work of fiction, *Who Is Virgil T. Fry?*, a short story about a high school teacher who lost favor with his colleagues because he taught so well.

Michener was born in 1907 in New York City and earned his bachelor's degree at Swarthmore College in 1929. As a teacher, he was attracted to what was then the Colorado State College of Education by the dynamic and innovative program in Progressive Education fostered by **George W. Frasier**, president. While at Greeley, Michener set up innovative courses for the secondary training school and taught social studies, contributing articles to professional publications and editing a landmark book, *The Future of the Social Studies*. He also acquired an MA degree while there and then took a year off to work on doctoral studies and teach at Harvard University. In 1942, he became associate editor of the McMillan Company, publishers of textbooks.

As a member of the U.S. Naval Reserve, he was called to active duty during World War II, and his Pacific service inspired the popular novel that led to instant fame. Since that time, he has published a multitude of works, including *Centennial*, a novel based on Colorado history. Among his most famous works are *Hawaii, Texas, Alaska, Poland, The Covenant, Fires of Spring,* and *Return to Paradise.* Michener's other honors include the U.S. Medal of Freedom and several honorary doctorates. The library at the Greeley university is named in his honor.

Popular Novelist of the Roaring Twenties...

Anne Parrish

Both of her parents were highly regarded artists in the stylish days when Colorado Springs was "Little London." Anne Parrish was born there in 1888 and was featured in the yearly Parade of Flowers, an idea of her father's which became a tradition in the Pike's Peak region during the "Gay Nineties."

Her background was in fashionable finishing schools: Ferris' School in Colorado Springs, and Hebb's School in Wilmington, Delaware.

Her bent was more to writing than art. She married Charles Corliss in 1915 and after her marriage began to write novels which became the rage of the "smart set" of the Twenties. Among these were *Pocketful of Posies* (1923), *Knee High to a Grasshopper* (1923), *The Perennial Bachelor* (1925), *Tomorrow Morning* (1926), *All Kneeling* (1928), and *Floating Island* (1930).

Corliss died in 1936, and Parrish married Josiah Titzell in 1938. When he died in 1943, she continued to live in retirement at her showplace home of Quantness, near Georgetown, Connecticut. It was there that she passed away in 1957.

Writer of Seventy Novels...

William McLeod Raine

Rider with the Arizona Rangers, correspondent for *American* magazine, writer of seventy novels and several reference works, as well as numerous short stories: that was the career of a man born in London, England, who ended up in Denver. Over ten million copies of his works have been published, with his famous brand, the circle WR, on most of them.

He was William McLeod Raine, born in 1871. His mother died when he was ten, and the family moved to Arkansas, where they set up a fruit and cattle farm. As Raine grew older, he worked with his father in the operation until the cattle were hit with "Texas fever." The family moved to Washington state, where Raine became a teacher, earning $36 a month. Later he won a Seattle position as principal and janitor at $70 a month. He obtained a degree from Oberlin College in 1894, and was a correspondent for the Chicago *Tribune* and the Cincinnati *Enquirer*. In Seattle he was a correspondent for the Seattle *Times* but was hit with the "white plague," tuberculosis, and, like so many other famous Coloradans, came to the state in 1898 to recover.

In Denver, he started as reporter for the Denver *Republican* but had to quit when the third floor walk to his desk could not be sustained by his diseased lungs. It was then that he began writing novels, starting with *The Luck of Eustace Blount*. As his health improved, he took jobs with the Denver *News, Post,* and *Times*. This led to a series of short stories based on the career of famous juvenile court judge **Ben Lindsey**. His wandering soul led him to Arizona, where he rode with the state troopers before he married and returned to Denver. His 1908 novel *Wyoming* initiated a long output of Westerns. He also wrote such noted non-fiction as *Famous Sheriffs and Western Outlaws* (1929), *Cattle* (1930), and *Guns of the Frontier* (1940).

Raine's settings were varied, but included such historic Western towns as Leadville, Butte, and Virginia City. He kept writing almost until the day of his death in 1954.

Founder of the *New Yorker* Magazine . . .

Harold Ross

His new trend in journalism became a fountainhead of creativity, introducing to the world such famous writers as Robert Benchley, Heywood Braun, James Thurber, Edna

Ferber, Robert Sherwood, and Dorothy Parker. The somewhat snobbish *New Yorker*, which became the ultimate determiner of literary standards for Gotham and the nation, was the brain child of Harold Ross, who founded it in 1925 and edited it until 1949.

Ross was born in Aspen in 1892. In 1899, his family moved to Salt Lake City, where he became a high school dropout, playing hookey to go to the library to read. When he wanted to quit school at the age of 14, his father refused permission. Ross ran away from home to Denver, obtaining a job as copy boy for the *Denver Post*. Later, he returned to Salt Lake City, working as a copy boy and then a reporter for the *Tribune*. A prodigious reader, observers claimed he was studying the most profound philosophers while still in his teens. The energetic reporter then worked for other Western newspapers, including several in California. He also spent short periods writing for papers in New Orleans and in Panama City.

With the advent of World War I, Ross joined the army, hoping to become an officer, but failed the examinations. In France, he went AWOL to Paris to seek a position with *Stars and Stripes* and, after much difficulty, was allowed to remain there. Working with then-Sergeant Alexander Wollcott, he rose to editorship.

Following the war, Marquis James founded the *American Legion Weekly* in Washington, D.C., and called in Harold Ross to edit the magazine. Ross married Jane Grant, a reporter for the *New York Times* stationed in Washington, and together they began to imagine a distinctive magazine for New York City.

The story of his hang-ups and his domineering but congenial nature has been written in many books and stories, and he became a legend of the American publishing world. He made his first trip back to Aspen in 1947 and was amazed to find his memory of a mining town bore little relationship to the modern ski resort. It was his last visit to Aspen, as he died in 1951.

Among his successes, he sometimes blundered in print, as when he claimed the Tenth Mountain Division, at Camp Hale near Leadville, was a sort of ski club which would spend World War II in a resort. The division was one of the most heroic and decorated fighting units of the war, and lost almost a thousand men in combat deaths.

Humorist for the Underworld . . .
Damon Runyon

The term "Runyonese" has been used in the literary world to describe the clever dialects and expressions of the New York underworld depicted in the novels of Damon Runyon. His stories, plays, and columns became some of the most popular writing of the first half of this century.

Born in Manhattan, Kansas, in 1884, Runyon moved to Pueblo, attending school until the age of fourteen, when he sneaked into the Spanish-American War as an Army enlistee. Runyon had already submitted articles to the Pueblo *Chieftain* and returned to serve as a reporter before moving to Denver to write for the *Rocky Mountain News*. By 1911, he found his way to the staff of the *New York American* and became a correspondent for the Hearst newspaper chain during World War I.

New York and its rich variety of lower-class types provided him with material which made them come to life in his columns, *Both Barrels* (1918-1936) and *The Brighter Side*, from 1937 until his death in 1946. Both columns were syndicated nationwide. He wrote about athletes, outlaws, ladies of questionable repute, and assorted show people.

Runyon's most famous book was *Guys and Dolls*, which became the famous Broadway musical comedy. Other works included *Blue Plate Special, Money From Home,* and *Take It Easy.*

He also wrote a play with Howard Lindsey, *A Slight Case of Murder*, and the movie scripts *Little Miss Marker* and *The Lemon Drop Kid.*

One of America's Greatest Humorists . . .

H. Allen Smith

Like so many early newspaper feature writers, H. Allen Smith moved all over the nation, spending several years with the *Rocky Mountain News* in Denver. His works were to lead to a series of hilarious books. He was acquainted with **Gene Fowler** and **Damon Runyon** in his Colorado days, and both Smith and Fowler developed reputations as light-hearted authors in later years.

Smith was born in McLeansboro, Illinois, in 1907. He began writing for the Huntington, Indiana, *Press* when he was only 15 years old. Later, he became a reporter in Tampa and Tulsa before discovering Colorado.

Among his most famous works are *Low Man on a Totem Pole, Life in a Putty Knife Factory, Lost in the Horse Latitudes,* and *To Hell in a Handbasket,* his autobiography.

H. Allen Smith's hilarity and mirth were accompanied by a subtle sense of the irony of human existence, a trait which made him a widely translated author of world fame before his death in 1976.

Academy Award Screenwriter . . .

Dalton Trumbo

To remark that Dalton Trumbo was controversial is certainly an understatement. A prolific writer of books, plays, and filmscripts, he turned out a novel which made Grand Junction flush with anger. He was an absolute pacifist when pacifism was considered un-American, and as a result he was blacklisted from Hollywood during the McCarthy witch-hunts of the 1950s. Undeterred, he continued to write screenplays under the *noms de plume* of Robert Rich and Sam Jackson.

Trumbo was born in Montrose in 1905 and moved as a small boy to Grand Junction, where his father worked as a shoe clerk. Graduating from high school there, he worked for a number of years as a reporter for the *Grand Junction Sentinel*, gaining ideas for his later work, in which the town always appeared as Shale City, Colorado. He spent a year at the University of Colorado and later picked up some college credits at the University of Southern California. In 1935, his first book, *Eclipse*, was published in England. It was a fictitious story based on thinly disguised characters in Grand Junction, where it produced pure outrage. The hilarious play *The Biggest Thief in Town* also had a Shale City setting.

The most shocking of his works, though, was *Johnny Got His Gun*, the horrifying story of a maimed victim of World War I. In his later years, Trumbo revised it into a movie based on the Vietnam War.

As a Los Angeles screenwriter, he wrote the scripts for *Hawaii, The Sandpiper, Exodus,* and *Spartacus*. His original creations included *Lonely Are the Brave, Papillion,* and *The Brave One*, which won the 1956 Academy Award. Since he was writing as Richard Rich, he was unable to receive it in his real name. After the passing of the 1950s, however, Trumbo was exonerated and his name removed from the blacklist. It had been placed there for his refusal to offer testimony which might implicate other Hollywood workers. Not until 1975 was the Oscar formally presented to him in his real name. He died the next year.

Novelist Who Influences World Opinions . . .

Leon Uris

His novel *Exodus* built world opinion in favor of the new nation of Israel and even changed some votes in the United Nations. Leon Uris has written much about the Jewish resettlement since World War II and has also covered many other fields, traveling to the sites to do on-the-spot research.

Born in Baltimore in 1924, he dropped out of school at the age of 17 to join the Marines during World War II. He moved to San Francisco after the war, where he became a carrier for the *Examiner*, working up to district manager for home delivery, and working on his first novel, *Battle Cry*.

Uris produced a number of best-sellers, including *Mila 18*, *Topaz*, *QB VII*, *Armageddon*, and *Mitla Pass*. Some of his works were made into movies; he hated the movie version of *QB VII*, and walked out on it. However, he helped in the production of *Battle Cry* and *Exodus*. The Broadway play *Ari* was a musical version of *Exodus*.

His third wife, Jill, is a successful Aspen photographer and the author of two non-fiction works on Ireland, featuring her fine pictures.

Leon Uris took up residence in Aspen in 1964. A skier, he also loves tennis and bowling. He and Jill lead private lives there, and he has continued his prodigious writing, using a style quite refined for a man who claims he failed English three times!

The Creator of Beanie Malone . . .

Lenora Mattingly Weber

Lenora Mattingly was born in Dawn, Missouri, in 1895. When she was twelve years old her family homesteaded on a ranch near Deer Trail, and she discovered the world of the West. Horses were her first love. In fact, she rode in the girls' events at the Cheyenne Frontier Days rodeo and her team won the blue ribbon in the girls' relay. Rodeo was a strong tradition around Deer Trail, where the first rodeo in history was held.

She attended high school in Denver, graduating from Manual High, where she fell in love with Albert Weber, a coach there. She eventually became his wife. Lenora did a little writing in her early years, including articles for the Catholic home magazine, *Extension*. These proved so popular that she began writing fiction for other popular magazines and, by the time she was thirty, she had begun a serious career in writing, mostly for children.

Her most famous series involved the adventures of the irrepressible teenaged Colorado ranch girl, Beanie Malone. These books were an instant success, but she also did other juvenile works such as *Riding High, Wind on the Prairie, Podgy and Sally, Coeds,* and *Rocking Chair Ranch.*

Starting with her first Beanie book, *Meet the Malones,* which Lenora wrote shortly after the sad death of her husband in 1941, she was one of the nation's most popular writers for children. A television series was based on the Beanie stories.

Lenora Mattingly Weber died in 1971, but her stories are still beloved by youth all over the nation. Her manuscripts are the subject of a special collection in the Denver Public Library.

The Poets

One of the First Famous "Cowboy Poets" ...

Austin Corcoran

Born in Pennsylvania in 1878, Austin Corcoran was one of ten children. His family moved to Grand Junction while he was a mere toddler, and, in his words, he "lived most of my life on the edge of civilization." He remembered the stage coach which served the town with a precarious run through DeBeque Canyon, a Hartford stage (with leather springs) driven by Billy Hamilton. While getting a sporadic education in Grand Junction, he was also a cowboy from the age of five on.

As a youth, Austin guided the survey party which named the Bookcliff formation. While on the Bookcliffs they found a rusty "Henry" rifle, and so named the nearby stream Rifle Creek; the stream later gave its name to the town of Rifle.

Corcoran took off for the Alaska Gold Rush at the turn of the century and then spent some time roping cattle in Hawaii and Mexico before returning to Grand Junction, where he established a homestead. In 1928, he sold his land and cattle and turned to a new career, writing short stories and poems as a "Cowboy Poet."

His first poem, "Chuck Time on the Roundup," had been published in 1915. Among his later poems which appeared in magazines and anthologies were "Silver Saddles," "Medicine Ranch," and "Walls of Thunder Creek." In his later days, he moved to Cañon City where he wrote a full volume of poetry entitled *Hidden Trails*. It was published in 1962, a short time before his death at the age of 87.

Wynken, Blynken and Nod's Creator . . .
Eugene Field

A sleepy-time rhyme still popular after more than a century, the *Dutch Lullaby* is more commonly known as *Wynken, Blynken and Nod,* composed by the man who edited the *Denver Tribune* in the early 1880s. Eugene Field wrote the poem for his little son, and later, when the boy died, he wrote the pathetic verse, *Little Boy Blue,* which began, "The little toy soldiers are covered with dust . . ."

During Field's short life (1850-1895), he worked for a number of newspapers after a New England boyhood and studied at Williams and Knox Colleges and the University of Missouri. When he lived in Denver, he was noted as a very witty practical joker. He was also a habitual drinker, keeping several "ink wells" on his desk filled with whiskey for "inspiration."

Field managed to get the famous writer Oscar Wilde, noted for his effeminate nature, to come to Colorado. When Wilde arrived, he was disappointed with size of the crowd there to greet him, as Field had already posed in a carriage parade, and the people thought they had seen the great Wilde. Field also invited Wilde to Leadville, site of the editor's summer cottage, where it was expected the rowdy miners would make short work of the esthete; however, Leadville welcomed Wilde warmly and inspired his tribute to the rugged West in a later work.

After leaving Colorado, Field went on to the Chicago *News*, where he spent the rest of his years. One of his most lasting poems during his Denver years was "Chipeta," a celebration of the famous wife of Ute Chief Ouray.

Poet of the Great American West...

Thomas Hornsby Ferril

His roots ran deep in the soil of the mountains and plains. His grandfather was an Army chaplain during the Indian Wars, and his father was city editor of the *Rocky Mountain News* during the late nineteenth century. His friend and admirer, Carl Sandburg, called him "one of the great poets of America." John Ciardi considered him one of the few truly major poets in the nation. Robert Frost wrote a verse honoring him.

Thomas Hornsby Ferril was born in Denver in 1896 and graduated from East High School and Colorado College before he joined the Army in World War I. After the war, he wrote for the *Denver Times* and then the *Rocky Mountain News*, where he was a movie and theater critic. In 1926, he became public relations director for Great Western Sugar Company, a job he retained for 42 years while writing for numerous publications. His articles and poems appeared in *Harper's* magazine, and he wrote a regular column for the *Rocky Mountain Herald*, which was edited by his wife, Helie. His poems were published by the *New Yorker* and *Atlantic*, and in 1936, he won the coveted Oscar Blumenthal prize established by *Poetry, A Magazine of Verse* for his monumental "Words for Leadville."

Ferril was honored in his own state when his verses were selected to accompany the famous paintings of **Allen True** in the rotunda of the State Capitol, and again, in his later years, by being named the state Poet Laureate.

His poem, "Cadetta" (the sound of wheels) was awarded the nation's first annual Robert Frost Poetry Award. He also won prizes from Doubleday Doran, the Forum Award, and the Academy of American Poets. He was recipient of the Ridgley Torrence Prize from the Poetry Society of America.

His books included *Words for Denver, I Hate Thursday*, and several collections of poems. "Magenta" was one of his masterpieces, later used as the theme of a television documentary about his career. His play *And Perhaps*

Happiness premiered at the Central City Opera House in 1958.

He continued to write in his later years and died in 1988 at the age of 92.

Railroad Bard of the Rockies . . .

Cy Warman

Cy Warman was probably most famous nationally for the musical rendition of his poem, "Sweet Marie," but he is remembered in Colorado for his famous poem, "Creede," which ends with the lines:

> Where it's day all day in the daytime
> And there is no night in Creede.

He wrote those lines during a brief stint as editor of Creede's *Daily Chronicle.*

Warman was born on a farm near Greenup, Illinois, in 1855 and learned to write in the local school. For a while, he worked with his father on the farm and then became a wheat broker in Pocahantas, Illinois. At age 25 he moved to Colorado, working in a smelter at Cañon City and then as a railway yard worker in Salida, where he married Myrtle Marie Jones, who was the inspiration for his famous poem and song. They had two children.

He then became a fireman and later an engineer for the Denver and Rio Grande Western Railway, which inspired so many of his poems and short stories. In 1888, he became editor of *The Western Railway,* a magazine published in Denver.

In the mid-1890s, Warman moved to the East to write for *The Century* and *McClure's* magazine, and his stories and poetry were recognized nationally. Among his poetic works was "Mountain Melodies," which came out in 1892. His prose works included "Tales of an Engineer" (1898), "Snow On The Headlight" (1899), "The Last Spike" (1908), and "Weiga of Temagani," tales of the Algonquin Indians, which was published in 1908.

Soon after that, the Warmans moved to London, Ontario, Canada, where he became seriously ill and died in 1914.

The Picture Makers
and Stone Carvers

Weaver Considered A National Treasure . . .

Eppie Archuleta

Her grandfather, Isidoro Martinez, was one of the famous weavers of Chimayo, New Mexico, and he passed the fine art of intricate blanket-making down to Eppie Archuleta. She cultivated it and brought it back to the San Luis Valley of Colorado, where the craft had almost been lost.

Eppie was born in 1922 at Santa Cruz, New Mexico, and at age eighteen married farmer Frank Archuleta. She toiled in the fields and raised children by day, weaving rugs and blankets by night. When they moved to Alamosa, she was credited with single-handedly revitalizing the Hispanic weaving tradition in that area.

Eppie worked with Adams State College and valley school districts to set up a program to teach the art to other adults. Her work both as an artist and as a teacher brought her the National Heritage Fellowship, the nation's highest award for traditional arts. The Smithsonian Institute put her work on permanent display and the National Endowment for the Arts proclaimed her a "national treasure."

Creator of Bloom County . . .

Berke Breathed

His satirical comic strip *Bloom County* won a Pulitzer Prize for editorial cartooning. It starred an ever-optimistic penguin named "Opus" and was carried in more than 950 newspapers. Berke Breathed, who was born in Los Angeles in 1957, moved to Houston at the age of 15 and finished high school there.

At the University of Texas he began doing a comic strip entitled *The Academic Waltz*, satirizing college life, and it became an immediate hit in the student newspaper.

After graduation, he created the cartoon strip which made him famous and soon was able to build his own hideaway at Evergreen, where he could view the foibles of modern civilization from a detached position. His work habits were unusual, to say the least. He would work 48 to 60 hours at a time, creating *Bloom County* episodes for two weeks of publication, then go enjoy the mountains or boating on Lake Powell in Utah. In 1986 he married photojournalist Jody Boyman.

Bloom County reaped wealth from its wide circulation, in addition to spin-offs in toys, clothing, and greeting cards. However, Breathed decided to end the series in 1989 with the comment that "a good comic strip is no more eternal than a ripe melon." With the the demise of *Bloom County*, though, Breathed turned his talents to a new comic strip, *Outland.*

Artist of the Old West . . .
Harold Edward Bryant

More than one nationally recognized art critic considered Harold Bryant to be in the same class with famous Western artists Frederick Remington and Charles Russell. His pictures of the early West, carefully based on the real costumes of pioneers, cowboys, miners, and Indians, were widely reproduced in such magazines as *Household, Capper's Farmer, Atlantic Monthly,* and *Fortune.*

He was born in Pickrell, Nebraska, in 1894 and moved to the Appleton suburb of Grand Junction in 1903, graduating from Appleton High School. After his graduation, Bryant went to Chicago to study at the Art Institute and became a commercial artist there.

Among his other interests was music. With the advent of World War I, he joined the field artillery and was assigned as a saxophonist for the unit band, then stationed in Kansas. When the unit went overseas, he went into combat and was gassed, but recovered in time to do some post-war touring of Europe and see the great masterpieces in the art museums there.

After returning to the United States, he continued his musical career, touring with a dance band for a few years before moving to New York to resume his career in commercial art. In addition to illustrative work for leading magazines, he created advertisements and collectors' pieces for the Seagram Distillery. The firm made framable copies of his work available to all who wrote in, and his prints of famous Western scenes hung in thousands of homes.

In 1940, he moved back to Grand Junction to continue his work. There he married Ruth, who played the violin. They enjoyed playing music together while he continued to produce his famous paintings until his death by cancer ten years later.

Self-Taught Pioneer Etcher of the Southwest . . .

George Elbert Burr

When he was only eleven years old, George Burr heard some table talk about the famed English etcher, Sir Francis Seymour Haden. Young George proceeded to cut a piece of zinc from the spark plate used to protect the floor beneath the kitchen stove, etched it, and printed it between the rollers of the family washing machine. So began his lifelong career.

Burr was born in Monroe Falls, Ohio, in 1859. As a youth, he worked in his father's hardware store and made etchings on copper from the tin shop there. In 1880, he took his savings and went to Chicago's Art Institute but stayed only 11 days, disgusted with the regimentation. However, his work was good enough to get him assignments for *Harper's* and *Leslie's* magazines when he and his wife, Elizabeth, moved to New York in 1888. The next year he was selected to accompany the inaugural tour of President Benjamin Harrison and had his first glimpse of the Southwest. Elizabeth's poor health prompted a move to Denver in 1906, and Burr opened a studio at 1325 Logan Street, making engravings and painting water-colors.

Denver, under the domineering and narrow-minded so-cially elite tastes of the time, failed to recognize him, but his fame spread throughout the nation, gradually reaching the point that almost every leading museum and art collection in the world owned some of his works. From his cabin at Eldorado Springs, he turned out two masterpieces, *Old Cottonwoods* and *The Sentinel Pine*.

Burr left Denver at age 66 and lived in Phoenix, Arizona, the rest of his life, gaining new fame for his plates of Arizona and New Mexico. He died in 1939.

Four Decades of Political Cartoons . . .

Paul Conrad

Paul Conrad got his start as a political cartoonist while working for the *Denver Post* from 1950 until 1964, winning for that newspaper its first Pulitzer Prize. His clever jibes at the American political scene won the coveted award in 1964, after which he moved to Los Angeles to continue his syndi-cated panels with the *Times*.

Conrad was born at Cedar Rapids, Iowa, in 1924. He served in World War II for four years. A sculptor as well as a cartoonist, he turned out commendable pieces, but it was his canny drawings that made him most famous, winning addi-tional Pulitzers in 1971 and 1984. During his four-decade ca-reer he has also written humorous books on politics: *The King and Us* and *Pro and Conrad*.

The Poultry Farmer Who Flourished with the Camera . . .

Laura Gilpin

She was a fine student of violin at New England Conservatory when she was still a teenager, but she loved the Brownie camera given to her on her twelfth birthday. Laura Gilpin, born in Colorado Springs in 1891, became one of the greatest American black-and-white picture makers, celebrated by the famous Ansel Adams. Her works are a feature in the Amon Carter Museum in Fort Worth, Texas.

In order to help rescue her family from financial disaster, Laura operated a poultry farm at Delta, Colorado, from 1912 until 1915, when she had saved enough to study at the Clarence H. White School of Photography. Her photographs soon won professional admiration throughout the nation. She was busy in Colorado as photographer for the Central City Opera Association, and she took many notable pictures of Denver and its architectural achievements.

Her greatest fame, however, came from her portraits of Indians and landscapes of the Southwestern deserts. Establishing her studio in Colorado Springs, she took leave to become Boeing Airplane Corporation's chief photographer during World War II. Moving to Santa Fe after the war, she produced her own books of photography and narrative: *The Pueblos, Temples in Yucatan,* and her masterpiece, *The Rio Grande: River of Destiny.*

Her Santa Fe home became a place of wonder for photographers studying her technique. She received an honorary doctorate from Colorado College, and in 1972 she was commissioned to do a study of Canyon de Chelly in Arizona.

Laura Gilpin never married. She died in 1979, but both her photographs and her books are treasured collectors' items throughout the world today.

The Father of Red Ryder and Little Beaver...

Fred Harman

A real cowboy artist—that was Fred Harman of Pagosa Springs. He not only turned out to be an expert in oil paintings but also created a nationally syndicated cartoon strip which ran in 750 newspapers and was the inspiration for forty movies.

Born in St. Joseph, Missouri, in 1902, Fred came to Pagosa at the age of two months, and it was there that he learned to be a cowboy. He eventually went to Kansas City, working in the press room of a newspaper. His ability in commercial art was recognized, and he went to work with a commercial art firm. This studio also employed Walt Disney, who became fascinated with the idea of animated cartoons and continued on his own in Hollywood. Fred married his love, Lola, and returned to Pagosa, cowpunching for forty dollars a month and painting some oils, now very valuable. By 1928, though, he was bankrupt.

In 1934, Harmon went all over the nation trying to market a comic strip called Bronc Peeler, but it was a bust. It wasn't until 1938, when he was in New York marketing his oils, that he hit upon the idea of Red Ryder and his side-kick, Little Beaver.

The success of his comic was phenomenal. It enabled Fred to buy his own ranch at Pagosa Springs. Other royalties came in from radio shows based on the script, movie rights, and such products as the Red Ryder Beebee Rifle.

He moved to Phoenix, Arizona, in the late 1970s after his strip had been dropped, but continued to produce his collectible oil paintings until his death in 1982.

The Commissioner Who Painted His Indian Friends ...

John Dare Howland

They called him "Captain Howland" after his service as a scout in the Indian wars of 1862 - 1864, and the name stuck when he was later appointed secretary of the Indian Peace Commission. He was Colorado's pioneer artist and became famous throughout the nation for his careful studies of "Black Kettle," or "Moketevata," as he preferred to call the portrait, and "Hunting Buffalo on the Plains."

Jack—he preferred the nickname—was born in 1843 at Zanesville, Ohio, the son of a riverboat captain. He left for the West at the age of 14, becoming a hunter and trader for the American Fur Company, dealing mostly with buffalo hides. His ability with native tongues gained him the acceptance of many of the tribal leaders, and they posed for him as he sketched their profiles for *Harper's Weekly* and *Frank Leslie's Magazine*. Howland also wrote articles to accompany those pictures, and the money earned as a correspondent enabled him to go to Europe for a formal education in art, instructed by such renowned artists as Charles Armand-Dumaresque.

Howland also learned the art of sculpture, and he designed the bronze statue which stands at the west entrance to the Colorado State Capitol. He was most noted, though, for his portraits and his landscapes, now gathered in museums world-wide.

He passed away in 1914, having stayed with the brush in Denver even during his sixties.

Pioneer Photographer of the West ...

William H. Jackson

America was enthralled by his photograph of the Mount of the Holy Cross, and reprints of it appeared in thousands of parlors. (Unfortunately, the formation lost its effect through natural rockfall during World War II.) William H. Jackson was both a photographer and a painter and was among the first to capture the grandeur of the Rockies on film.

He was born at Keesville, New York, in 1843. At the age of seventeen, he took part in the Civil War and noted later that "all talk about the glory and chivalry of war is poppy-cock babbling of fictionalists."

Fascinated with the camera, he traveled through Nebraska, both to take some outstanding photographs of the land and people and, in some cases, to do watercolor paints of the region. His numerous paintings remain on display at several locations along the old Oregon Trail.

In the early Seventies, Jackson was taking photographs for the Union Pacific Railroad to promote tourism when he was appointed official photographer for the famed F.V. Hayden's surveys of the West (1873-80). He lugged his equipment to the tops of mountains. A mule carried his chemicals, glass plates, and portable darkroom, which he erected on the spot. The wet collodion process used at the time required that the plate be exposed and developed before it dried, or it would be ruined.

In 1880, he settled in Denver, opening a studio on Larimer Street, and ran a successful business for two decades before moving to Detroit. Retiring in the 1920s, he lived to be almost a hundred years old, succumbing in 1943. He donated a large collection of his original plates, including the first photographs of Mesa Verde, to the Colorado Historical Society.

Another Pulitzer Cartoonist . . .

Patrick Bruce Oliphant

In 1958, the International Federation of Free Journalists awarded Australian political cartoonist Pat Oliphant second place as the funniest cartoonist in the world. He went on a world tour to study technique and fell in love with Denver. There he met **Paul Conrad** of the *Denver Post*, whose position as editorial cartoonist he took in 1964 when Conrad moved to California.

Oliphant was born in Adelaide, Australia, in 1935. As a young man he worked as copy boy and then as press artist for the *Adelaide Advertiser*. In 1955 he became the cartoonist for the paper, working there until moving to Denver.

Oliphant's works, trademarked by a witty little penguin in the corner, won a 1967 Pulitzer Prize. His works were syndicated within a year of his arrival in the U.S., and he continued at the *Post* until taking a post with the *Los Angeles Times* in the early 1970s.

The Master of Heroic Sculpture ...
Alexander Phimister Proctor

His "Bronco Buster" and "On The War Trail" grace the Denver Civic Center. "The Pioneer Mother" still inspires Kansas City. "The Circuit Rider" is a centerpiece at Stanford University. His statue of Theodore Roosevelt stands in Portland, Oregon. Several of his sculptures stand in the nation's capital, and others beautify cities around the world.

Alexander Proctor, or "Phimis," as they called him, was fourteen years old when his family moved to Denver. Born in Ontario, Canada, in 1860, he also had lived in Michigan, where he had shown a natural talent for art. Finding the city life of pioneer Denver too confining, the family moved to Grand Lake, where his father became a big game hunting guide and taught Phimis about wild animals. There the youth shot a bear and was fascinated by its powerful body. He had attended Arapahoe School in Denver but sought a career in art. He moved to New York City, where he attracted the attention of artist J. Harrison Mills with a drawing of a panther. His first major sculpture, "Cowboy," was a stunning feature of the 1893 Chicago World's Fair and won him national attention.

Proctor didn't limit himself to sculpture. He made wood engravings for books and later turned to copper etching. His masterpieces in Denver were created in 1920 and 1921, after he had returned to the Colorado Rockies he loved so well. Later, as a resident of Pendleton, Oregon, he sculpted another famous work, "The Western Sheriff," which still stands there. He won practically every award and honor available here and abroad for his statues, all in the heroic tradition. During his declining years, Proctor maintained homes in La Mesa, California, Seattle, Washington, and New York City. He died in Palo Alto, California, in 1950.

Pulitzer Prize Photographer . . .

Tony Suau

A poignant Memorial Day photograph of a woman hugging her husband's gravestone at Fort Logan Cemetery won the Pulitzer Prize for Tony Suau, a young member of the *Denver Post* staff.

A native of Peoria, Illinois, Suau graduated from the Rochester Institute of Technology and at the age of 27 moved to Denver to work for the *Post*.

An assignment in Ethiopia led to awards for a touching picture of starvation. Portraits which wring the emotional heart of the viewer are his specialty.

His Memorial Day picture won the 1984 Pulitzer Prize for photography. It was the third Pulitzer for the *Post*, the other two having been awarded for the editorial cartooning of **Paul Conrad** and **Pat Oliphant**.

The West's Foremost Muralist . . .

Allen Tupper True

Allen True became nationally famous as a muralist, with his paintings gracing the Colorado, Missouri and Wyoming state capitols as well as many other public buildings in the West. He was admitted to the Royal Society of Arts, England's most renowned art society, a rare honor for an American. The American Federation of the Arts sponsored a 29-city nation-wide tour of his works.

- Born in Colorado Springs in 1881, he moved to Denver shortly thereafter and graduated from Manual Training High School. After two years of study at the University of Denver, he transferred to the Corcoran Art School in Washington, D.C., where he studied under the famous Howard Pyle. He was employed in London as an assistant to Frank Brangwyn, one of the world's master muralists.

True did illustrations for *Scribner's, Harper's* and the old *Life* magazine from his studio near Sloan's Lake in Denver. His interest in color led him to become a consultant to the federal government, introducing the concept of painting machinery in bright colors to create a more congenial atmosphere and promote greater safety. He worked with engineer **John Savage** to design both the color schemes and decorations for the plants at the Boulder (Hoover), Grand Coulee, and Shasta dams. He assisted in the restoration of the Colorado National Bank Lobby in Denver and uncovered the original decorations at the old Central City Opera House and Teller House.

His Memorial Center murals at the University of Colorado in Boulder were abandoned when the center was remodeled in 1964, but **Buck Burshears** rescued them for the Koshare Kiva in La Junta.

More lasting, though, are his great murals in the rotunda of the Colorado Capitol in Denver, accompanied by the poetry of **Thomas Hornsby Ferril**.

True was married to Emma Goodman but divorced in 1934. He died in 1955.

Pioneer of American Wildlife Photography . . .

Allen Grant Wallihan

The tiny hamlet of Lay, in northwest Colorado, was home to one of the nation's first photographers of wild animals in their natural habitat. Born in 1859 at Footville, Wisconsin, A.G. Wallihan moved with his family to the Denver area in 1870, and later joined the silver boom at Leadville. There he married the lady who would be his inspiration, partner, and yokemate in photography. She was always identified simply as Mrs. Wallihan. Seeking freedom from the chaotic "civilization" of Leadville, they wandered to the Federal Supply Camp of Lay, in what is now Moffat County. At that time, it was virgin plains country, teeming with wildlife.

Mrs. Wallihan bought a camera from an itinerant missionary, and together they learned to load it with dry plates, eventually handling their own darkroom work in that isolated land. By 1888, they could get close enough to deer to catch them on film and learned to stalk the other wildlife in the region, becoming hunters with the lens. For a half century they pursued this hobby while maintaining the Lay post office.

Their photographs attracted national attention in 1894 with the publication of the book *Hoofs, Claws and Antlers of the Rocky Mountains*, complete with an introduction by Theodore Roosevelt. It was reissued in 1902 with an introduction by William F. "Buffalo Bill" Cody. Another work, *Camera Shots at Big Game,* also bore Roosevelt's blessing, this time as President. Famed naturalist William T. Horaday claimed that Americans owed a greater debt to Wallihan than to any other man of his time, although his books always showed the author-artists as "Mr. and Mrs. A.G. Wallihan."

Their most famous picture was of a cougar leaping from a tree toward Mr. Wallihan. His techniques kept pace with improved modern equipment, and he became a model for later followers of the art of natural photography. He died in 1935, but not until he had lovingly sculptured caskets for himself and his wife. Mrs. Wallihan died soon afterward.

The Teachers

Reformer of American High Schools ...

James Hutchins Baker

Possibly the most influential president the University of Colorado ever had was classical scholar James H. Baker, whose "Committee of Ten" led the revision of curriculum in secondary schools from the traditional studies designed only for college aspirants to more broad-ranging and vocational instruction. He has been ranked with the famous Charles Eliot of Harvard and Nicholas Murray Butler of Columbia as innovators in American education.

Born in Harmony, Maine, in 1848, Baker graduated from Bates College in 1873 and taught school in that area before coming to Denver as principal of East High School in 1875. His work there was innovative and drew national attention even before he was named president of the University of Colorado in 1892. During his tenure at the university, the enrollment grew from 100 to 1,300, and the campus from one to 25 buildings. However, it was his presidency of both the National Council of Education and the National Association of State Universities that led to his fame. Writing numerous books on both high school and college education, he founded the Committee of Ten to lead high schools in the preparation of students for interested and involved lives whether or not they went on to college. Careful research proved that they did as well in college as they had under the antiquated programs of the nineteenth century. He also proposed a national university system and established a program of time conservation in which students could take more courses within the same period of preparation.

Baker continued scholarship in his own fields, Latin and Greek. He enjoyed the family ranch at Arvada and retired there in 1914 after 22 years at the helm of the University. At his death in 1925 he was working on the last of a three-volume history of Colorado.

America's Most Famous Scoutmaster . . .

James Francis "Buck" Burshears

It was in 1933 that Buck Burshears conceived the idea of making Boy Scout Troop 10 in La Junta into a group dedicated to the study and preservation of American Indian lore. Since then, it has become the most famous troop in the nation, performing dances that even some native tribal leaders have come to study to recover their lost traditions. The Koshare Indians (Koshare means fun-maker) have become a model for the entire scouting program, with over 500 Eagle ranks awarded during the years of Burshears' leadership.

Buck was born in Swink in 1909 and later moved to La Junta, where he attended high school before enrolling at Colorado College and doing further work in sociology at St. Louis University. He was a social worker and railroad contractor, but his fame rested on his 65 years of work with the Boy Scouts of America.

As a college student, he became very interested in Indian lore, and studied with some of the nation's leading experts on the subject. Teaching the boys the dances, Burshears gave them a basis for the unique program of performances; they made all of their own costumes and props, giving attention to absolute authenticity. He married Jane White in 1949, and she became the troop "mother" until her death in 1971.

One of the great achievements of this man, who received presidential citations for his work, was the establishment of the Koshare Kiva in La Junta, featuring a collection of art worth millions of dollars and now a popular tourist attraction. Much of the art was donated by Burshears himself. His inspiration to thousands of scouts, both in his own troop and nationwide, was contained in his admonition, "Don't wait to become a great man; be a great boy!"

Buck continued to lead the troop until his death in 1987.

The First American Saint . . .
Mother Frances Xavier Cabrini

On Lookout Mountain above Denver stands a shrine dedicated to the memory of the first American ever canonized by the Roman Catholic Church, Frances Cabrini, who spent a part of her busy life establishing an orphanage and school in Denver. She was born in 1850 in Italy and yearned from childhood for a missionary career.

Mother Cabrini first received church attention when she volunteered her nursing skills during an Italian smallpox epidemic. In 1880 she was directed to found an order of sisters devoted to missionary work, which she started in an abandoned Franciscan monastery.

Her work brought her to New York in 1889, and she became a naturalized American citizen, founding in the New World 67 institutions, including convents, schools, hospitals, and orphanages.

In 1902 her order rented a small house at the corner of Palmer Street and 34th Avenue in Denver and began a school. Impoverished parents paid 25 cents a month tuition. Mother Frances herself came to Denver to establish an orphanage and resided in the city from 1905 until 1912, although she was constantly checking up on other projects throughout the country during that time.

Her dream, not completed until after her passing in 1917, was the Queen of Heaven Memorial School at 4825 Federal Boulevard. Her achievement was of such magnitude that the Church received special dispensation from Pope Pius XI to set aside the rule that 50 years must elapse before examination for sainthood, and the ultimate honor was conferred in 1946.

One of America's Foremost Mathematicians . . .

Florian Cajori

As did so many noted Coloradans, Florian Cajori came to this state for his health, with an incipient case of tuberculosis. The higher altitude and dry atmosphere of Colorado Springs brought him to Colorado College in 1888, and he attained a reputation among the mathematicians of the world which was to make his writings standard texts in the field.

Born in St. Aignan, Switzerland, in 1859, Cajori came to the United States in 1875 and within a decade was a senior professor of physics at Tulane University. However, when he contracted the dread "white plague," President William F. Slocum of Colorado College welcomed him to the faculty as a physicist. His interest in physics, though, led him deeper into the study of mathematics in its most advanced forms and into the development of the entire field. In 1898 he became a mathematics professor and served in that capacity and as dean of the engineering department. Cajori left the college in protest when Slocum resigned in a dispute with the governing body in 1918.

He continued his career as professor of the history of mathematics at the University of California, Berkeley. He wrote *The History of Mathematics* and *The History of Mathematical Notations*, both standard texts in the field, as well as other books and numerous professional articles. Cajori died in 1930.

The Son of Progressive Education . . .

George Willard Frasier

Philosopher John Dewey of Columbia University has often been called "the father of Progressive Education," the concept which revolutionized teaching methods in the twentieth century. His protégé was George Willard Frasier, who at age 33 became the youngest college president in the nation when he was appointed head of Colorado State College of Education, now known as the University of Northern Colorado, in Greeley.

Frasier, born in Michigan in 1890, was a gifted educator with degrees from the State Normal School in Michigan, Stanford University, and Columbia Teachers' College. He served at the State Teachers' College in Cheney, Washington, and for the Denver Public Schools before arriving in Greeley in 1923 as Dean of the Graduate College. Frasier did innovative studies critical of traditional teaching and promoting Dewey's ideas, including "learning by doing," getting students to enjoy school, and the assignment of responsibility: "If the student hasn't learned, the teacher hasn't taught." He was appointed president of the college in 1924.

During the course of his career, Frasier made the college at Greeley one of three leaders in the new movement which would eventually dominate American education, joining Peabody College and Columbia itself. His powerful textbook *An Introduction to Education* was used in teacher-training institutions nationwide. He also found time to produce textbooks on the literature of education, social studies, finance, and spelling. Probably most important of all, the versatile and innovative leader attracted to Colorado some of the most famed writers and instructors in the new Progressive Education movement, including such talented "doers" as soon-to-become-famous novelist **James Michener**.

According to his successor, William R. Ross, Frasier was a "human dynamo . . . brilliant . . . full of energy, full of pep, full of drive." Above all, however, he was a man who inspired the teachers of America to think philosophically. Frasier led the college until 1947 and continued to teach there and at Stanford University.

Pioneer in Adult Career Education . . .
Emily Griffith

Before Emily Griffith, Denver's unique and imaginative schoolmistress, developed the idea of special schools where adults could learn vocational skills and languages, such training was available only in limited night classes. The concept of her Opportunity School, which admitted anyone regardless of level of education, spread to other cities in America once she had established its value. Drop-outs could earn high school diplomas, immigrants could learn English, men and women could learn skills for better jobs, and they could study on their own schedules, either during the day or in the evening.

A native of Ohio, she was born in 1880 and taught in Nebraska before coming to Denver in 1895. She realized that learning should not end with youth must but be a lifetime pursuit. After much difficulty convincing community leaders, she established the Opportunity School in 1915 and became its first principal.

Griffith's dedication to the project was what made it famous. She was able to help many of her students get their first real jobs. There were beginning courses in the "Three R's" as well as vocational woodworking, sheet metal, mechanics, secretarial, nursing, sewing, and many other skills. During the first World War, her school trained men and women for specialized military tasks.

When she retired in 1933, the Denver Public Schools named the institution in her honor, and it continues its useful function to this day, still a national model.

Emily Griffith was victim of one of Colorado's most notorious unsolved murders. On June 19, 1947, her body was found at her Pinecliffe cabin. She had been shot to death.

The Scholar Who Warned America . . .

George Norlin

Returning to the United States after a year as an exchange scholar in Germany during the early 1930s, George Norlin pleaded with Americans to take notice of the horrifying direction of Nazism under the dictatorship of Adolph Hitler. Some listened, but most stayed in a comfortable isolationist frame of mind, concerned with economic problems at home. His books *Hitler: Why and Whither?* and *Fascism and Citizenship* raised the spectre of World War II.

Norlin was president of the University of Colorado. A native of Concordia, Kansas, he graduated from and taught at Hastings College in Nebraska and then studied at the University of Chicago, where he earned his doctorate in classical languages and joined the faculty. He married Minnie Dutcher in 1904 and they came to Boulder, where he joined the faculty of the university. He was appointed acting president in 1917 and in 1919 was named president, a position he held during two decades of dynamic growth and change in the institution. Among other achievements, he founded the Medical School in Denver. He stepped into the hot waters of political friction many times and fought the growing problem of athletic abuses in the nation's colleges, citing the trend for higher education to "prostitute its values" for notoriety in sports. One of his books was *Integrity in Education*.

Retiring in 1939, Norlin wrote his autobiography, *Things in the Saddle*. He died only 27 hours after the passing of his wife, Minnie, on March 31, 1942. *The Quest of American Life*, his last work, was published posthumously.

The Planners and
Builders

The World's Leading Traffic Engineer . . .

Henry A. Barnes

It was *Life* magazine that designated Henry Barnes "the world's leading traffic engineer" after this remarkable man, who quit school at age 15, had established an entirely new system for urban traffic in America. Hank, as he liked to be called, was born in 1906 in Newark, New York, and went to work as a railroad section hand after finishing the eighth grade. Later, he drove a bus to Florida on "the sucker run," selling people on buying land in that state's infamous real estate fiasco of the Twenties. After that he apprenticed as an electrician and made it to journeyman when he moved to Flint, Michigan, in 1926.

He became an auto worker and policeman there, but in 1931 an accident left him with a broken neck, a paralyzed arm, and a family to feed. His wife Hazel and their four children survived on what he could make building furniture and novelties of wood, until, in 1938, he was made Flint's traffic signal engineer. In the meantime, he kept picking up courses in night school to learn about all phases of engineering. His success was outstanding; he was one of the rare individuals who, despite his lack of a college degree, received a year's fellowship to the Yale School of Traffic Engineering. This led to his employment as Denver's traffic engineer in 1944.

He made bold changes to adjust the city to the era of heavy traffic: one-way streets, limited turns, and the famous "Barnes Dance" which halted all autos at downtown intersections while pedestrians could cross at all angles. By 1953, he had become famous and Baltimore hired him away from Denver; he upset them, too, by removing many statues from streets to parks. In the meantime he had developed computerized traffic lights which could keep traffic moving at steady speeds.

Then he went to New York City, site of the world's worst traffic jams, and set up programs which won him world-wide fame. He found time to write an autobiography, *The Man with the Red and Green Eye*. Barnes died of a heart attack in 1967 at the age of 61.

Colorado's Famous Tunnel Digger and Inventor ...

David Brunton

Engineers with the American and Italian armies used the Brunton Transit to survey their tunnel into Austria during World War I, and it soon became the tool used by engineers all over the world. It replaced a whole bagful of instruments for reconnaissance surveys. David Brunton invented the transit to help him with Colorado engineering problems, but it was only one of his thirty inventions.

Born in Ontario, Canada, in 1849, he served as an apprentice mining engineer in Toronto, coming to the United States in 1873 to study geology and chemistry at the University of Michigan. He also became a U.S. citizen and arrived in Colorado to pursue his calling in 1875. After constructing three mining mills in Georgetown, he went to Leadville in 1879, which was, in his words, "probably the wildest and wickedest boom town America has ever known." There he developed mines for **Meyer Guggenheim** and other moguls and formed his own corporation. He also found a wife, Katherine Kembel, who had come out from New York. After a term in Montana planning Marcus Daly's Anaconda Mine in Butte, he returned to Colorado, where he drove the Cowenhoven Tunnel, two and one half miles in length, to drain the Smuggler Mine at Aspen. It was the longest tunnel in the West at that time.

Brunton also designed the Laramie-Poudre Tunnel at Home and the Connaugh Tunnel on Rogers Pass. In the midst of all this, he found time to write two books, one on safety and the other on modern methods of tunneling, was president of the American Institute of Mining and Metallurgical Engineers, and was one of the few Americans elected to membership in the British Institute of Civil Engineers. During World War I, he served as a "dollar-a-day" volunteer consultant to the Navy.

Brunton created a number of inventions to bring electrical improvements to the mining industry, and at the age of 77 he was chairman of the board which drove the Moffat Tunnel, six miles long and the longest at that time in America. A hobbyist with automobiles and photography, he survived a terrible crash at Poudre River in 1910, one which killed his companion. He was the father of two boys, both of whom became engineers.

David Brunton died in 1927, still creating new ideas in tunneling and mining technology.

Harmonizing with Nature . . .

Burnham F. Hoyt

Denver's beautiful Red Rocks Amphitheater was designated by New York's Museum of Modern Art as one of fifty outstanding examples of American architecture. It won many other citations for Burnham Hoyt, the architect who carried into reality this dream of Denver parks manager George Cranmer, father of the city's Mountain Parks system.

Hoyt was born in Denver in 1887, graduated from North High School, and, after studying at the Beaux-Arts Institute in New York City, joined his brother Merrill in their own design company. During World War I, he worked as a camouflage designer overseas. On his return, he designed the charming St. Martin's Chapel at St. John's Cathedral in Denver as well as Lake Junior High School and the Denver Press Club building. He was a creative artist, refusing merely to copy existing styles for their own sake, a common practice of his era. He aimed at the setting and the style which fitted the environment. For some time, he was on assignment for John D. Rockefeller, designing New York's Riverside Church in Morningside Heights. Returning to Denver, he married Mildred Fuller and continued to create fine buildings.

The epitome of his work was the Red Rocks outdoor theater, which blends the natural setting and acoustics into one of the world's most pleasing combinations of man's design and nature's beauty. Birds would sit in the rocks and sing along with Lily Pons and the Denver Symphony.

Hoyt died in 1960.

Disarming the Widow-Maker . . .
John George Leyner

He was the first white child born in Boulder County, making his appearance August 20, 1860, a mile from the mouth of Left Hand Canyon. Forty-three years later, he invented the water drill for mining, saving the lives of many thousands of hard rock miners during the twentieth century.

J. George, as he was usually called, worked in Colorado mines most of his life, inhaling the dust which resulted in silicosis for so many of his cohorts. It was almost an axiom that if a man used the air-compressor drill long enough, he would get a fatal residue of rock dust in his lungs. Earlier hammer-and-drill teamwork had many dangers, but the new and speedier power drills were so lethal that they were called "widow-makers." The result was often called "miners' con" because the symptoms and deterioration were similar to those of tuberculosis, one of the dread diseases of that era, generally referred to as "consumption."

Leyner was an inventor as well as a miner. He experimented with several power drills and constantly faced frustration in the design of one that would produce less dust. He did come up with a drill which rotated as it drove, hammered by steam power. This sped up the process but still threw a constant backfire of dust at the drillers.

By 1903, he had discovered a whole new principle for the drill. Water was forced through a hole bored in the center of the drill bit, dampening the granules of rock and causing them to flow in a muddy mass from the drill-hole. His Leyner Engineering Works, near Littleton, produced this drill for mines all over the world. While silicosis was still a danger to miners, especially with the use of dynamite for blasting, the job of a hard rock miner was no longer a guaranteed death sentence.

The Man Who Electrified the World . . .
Lucian L. Nunn

The great Thomas Edison said it would never work. George Westinghouse thought it might and succeeded in lighting a few Eastern villages with alternating current (AC), but he still lacked a motor to produce AC on a steady basis. It would take the brilliance of L.L. Nunn to turn the discovery of Nicholas Tesla into a practical operation. The use of water power at the Ames station near Telluride made that town the first totally electrified community in the world.

L.L. Nunn was a man of short stature, standing only five feet, one inch tall. An obsession with the "Little Corporal," Napoleon, drove him to identify his own stature with the accomplishments of that empire-builder.

He was born on a prosperous farm near Cleveland in 1853, the ninth of eleven children. Nunn was a graduate of Cleveland Academy and went abroad, studying law in Germany. Upon his return to the United States, he studied more law in Massachusetts and sat in on lectures at Harvard, but by 1880, he still had no real occupation, and it was then that he drifted out to Telluride.

Nunn finally was admitted to the Colorado Bar in 1881 and set up a law practice specializing in mining. By 1888, he controlled a Telluride bank and had interests in several mines and downtown store buildings. The costs of electrical operations of mines were gigantic; the Gold King Mine alone shelled out $2,500 a month for its direct current system. Then the well-read Nunn went back to New York and met with Westinghouse, explaining that a water-powered generator at the mountain village of Ames could give continuous AC power. Westinghouse was reluctant, but Nunn pledged all of his holdings in support of the principle. The plant was built in 1890 and by 1891 the mines and the entire community were electrified from that one generator. The Gold King's costs for electricity dropped to only $500 a month!

Brilliant technicians came running to Telluride, where the Telluride Institute at Ames was established. Locals called these talented engineers "pinheads," but the scientists proved their abilities when, threatened with a flood from a broken dam, they used their slide rules to calculate that the waters would not quite reach the plant and stayed calm. The waters rose to exactly the level they had predicted.

Nunn moved on to establish the famous Ontario works at Niagara Falls. Lucian Nunn never married; when he died he left as a legacy the Telluride Institute at Cornell University in Ithaca, New York, and Deep Springs, a self-help school for boys in Nevada.

The "Billion Dollar Beaver" . . .
John Lucian Savage

He was called the "biggest dam designer in the world." John Savage was the chief design engineer for the U.S. Bureau of Reclamation during the era of big dams, and he designed most of them, including Grand Coulee, Hoover, Shasta, Norris and Imperial.

Born in 1880 in Wisconsin, he was a graduate of the University of Wisconsin and began his service as an engineer with the government in 1903 at Boise, Idaho. He took a few years off to do private consulting, but in 1916 he became the chief of design for Bureau of Reclamation structures, with his headquarters in Denver, where he spent the rest of his career. His design of the Boulder Dam on the Colorado River, later renamed Hoover Dam, was considered one of the seven wonders of the modern world when it began storing water in 1936. It won him an honorary doctorate from his alma mater.

Savage's fame spread world-wide, and he made trips around the globe, advising nations on the design of their own reclamation projects. When Australia's great Burrinjuck Dam was threatened with collapse in 1939, he was called in to save it. He even helped design the Panama Canal and the Madden Dam in Panama. South America, China, Nepal, and Afghanistan all planned projects based on his designs.

Interior Secretary **Oscar Chapman** referred to Savage's work as "the greatest structures in the world . . . everlasting monuments to his engineering skill."

Savage married his first wife, Jessie, in 1918. She died in 1940, and he married again, this time Olga Miner, from Seattle. In his later years, he was still advising on the various projects, including Colorado's Green Mountain Dam. As a hobby in his retirement, John built pianos. He was an octogenarian at the time of his death.

Inventor of the Electric Tramway . . .

Sydney Howe Short

Denver had the first operating electric tramway in the world. It appeared on the Colorado Seminary campus, located at Fourteenth and Arapahoe, in 1885, the brainchild of Sydney Short, vice president and chairman of the physics department at the Seminary, a secondary school which became the University of Denver the following year.

Short was born in 1838 in Ohio and made his way through several Eastern scientific schools before taking over the science department of the Denver school in 1880. He was enthralled by the power of electricity and built a circular track trolley on the campus, which he christened the "John Henry." It worked with a middle "hot line" such as is used by modern subway systems; however, the danger of injury meant most of the line had to be buried, making it inefficient, especially in wet weather. However, Short expanded with a line which ran up Colfax Avenue to Pennsylvania, across to Fifteenth Street, and then down to Center, a former downtown street. Heavy rains made the tramway inoperable, but the first thrust into a great idea had been made.

Sydney Short then moved on to St. Louis where he tried again, encountering the same problems until he converted the electric supply system to overhead wires. The system was force to use direct current (DC) until **Lucian Nunn**, in Telluride, proved the practicality of AC.

Short went on to establish a streetcar system for Cleveland and then was called to London, where he established the English Electrical Manufacturing Company, the first London trolley system to move by power other than horses.

In his career, he registered more than 500 patents, mostly related to electric transportation. Short died in 1902 after an attack of appendicitis.

He Dreamed of a Presidential White House in Colorado . . .

John Brisben Walker

Born near Pittsburgh, Pennsylvania, in 1845, John Walker had attended West Point and become a soldier of fortune by the age of twenty, when he was a general in the Chinese army. He arrived in Denver five years later, making millions in real estate promotions.

He designed Denver's first great amusement park, Riverfront, which covered much of the area of the Union Station and was anchored by his magnificent personal castle. He experimented in alfalfa cultivation with large acreages at Berkeley Lake and Rocky Mountain Lake and supervised the development of Highland Park in north Denver. Walker donated the land for the campus of Regis College and then left Denver for a colorful stint as editor of the Washington, D.C., *Chronicle*. Then he bought the ailing *Cosmopolitan* magazine and made it one of the nation's foremost publications, selling it to William Randolph Hearst in 1905 for $400,000.

He returned to Colorado many times. In 1900 he nursed an automobile up to the 11,000-foot elevation on Pike's Peak, the highest any automobile had been driven at the time, a jaunt which inspired later roads to the summits of that peak and Mount Evans. After moving back to Colorado, he was an influential promoter of the Denver Mountain Parks concept, working with famous Denver mayor Robert Speer.

To further his promotions, he built a castle near Morrison, atop Mt. Falcon. It was there he began work on a fantastic cliff side palace, complete with turrets, to serve as a summer White House for American presidents, but he was unable to persuade the federal government to help in the financing. When lightning struck his own mansion, he saw the dream die. Walker died penniless in 1931, but Falcon Park (in the Jefferson County Open Space system) still holds the remains of the ruined castle for all to see.

The Kokomo Innovator ...

Arthur R. Wilfley

Deep beneath a gigantic tailings pond near Climax, Colorado, stands the inundated remains of what was once the thriving mining camp named Kokomo. And it was in Kokomo that a young Missourian named Arthur Redman Wilfley conceived a new mill operation which would make possible the recovery of almost twice the gold previously extracted in milling operations and even made it possible to re-mill the tailings from earlier mining operations. It became famous the world over simply as the "Wilfley Table."

Born in the "show-me" state in 1860, Arthur came to Colorado at the age of eighteen to work in the mines and do some prospecting on his own. He learned the arts of the assayer and also gained a practical knowledge of engineering. In 1886, he drove a tunnel into the low level of the Seare Gulch Ridge and broke into veins which became the "Aftermath" and "White Quail" lodes.

Miners were penalized for sending ore to the smelters which still had mixtures of lead and zinc with the gold or silver. Wilfley worked with dozens of designs to get the heavier elements to separate on the riffle tables and finally came up with a sand table that did the job, letting only the valuable concentrates dance off the end of the platform. Manufactured in Denver and London, the Wilfley Table was such a boon to mining that it raised hopes even for operators who had nothing but tailings left from earlier processes.

Suffering from a heart problem, he moved to Denver with his family but continued developing such inventions as a new pump design. By 1924, he had 24 patents in his name. His sons George and Elmer took over management of his company. He passed away in 1927, leaving a legacy of innovation to the miners of the world.

The Merchants

The Stowaway Who Brewed the Beer . . .

Adolph Coors

The name is now famous as one of the nation's greatest beers. Its beginnings in 1873 originated with the innovative German, Adolph Coors, who was born in 1847 in Prussia. The son of a miller, Coors was apprenticed to a brewer but when faced with draft into the dread Prussian Army in 1868, he became a stowaway, settling in Chicago, where he served as a fireman, stonecutter, and bricklayer for several years. In 1872, he moved to Denver, where he was a gardener. The next year he bought an interest in an existing Golden brewery and soon bought out his partner. His expertise in the art made him an immediate success, and before long he was shipping his brew by wagon as far away as Leadville.

Coors married his girlfriend, Louise, in 1879, and they had two sons and three daughters.

When visiting his native land in 1914, the family was trapped by the Kaiser's government during the outbreak of World War I but, after many difficulties, was finally allowed to return to the United States.

Because of dissatisfaction with existing glass bottles, he started his own bottle works, changing to the production of porcelain ovenware and pottery in 1910. The material produced there was later used in attempts to "disintegrate atoms" at the University of Chicago, finally performed by scientist Enrico Fermi in 1942. During the prohibition years, Coors adapted the plant to the production of malted milk, making it one of the nation's greatest producers of that delicacy.

He fell from a building in Virginia in 1929 and died as a result of the injuries.

His sons Herman and Adolph, Jr., continued the brewery operation. Adolph, Jr., was the subject of a kidnapping plot which was foiled in the 1930s, but Adolph III, his grandson, was not so fortunate, being kidnapped and murdered in 1960.

Later developments in the Coors operation led to the development of Moravian barley as an agricultural crop in Colorado, and some claim it is the key to the popularity of the beer.

From Durable Treads to Learjets ...

Charles Cassius Gates, Sr.

One of Colorado's most famous industries, world-wide, is the Gates Corporation, the world's largest manufacturer of power transmission belts and hoses for industrial applications. It grew from a small organization founded by Charles Gates in 1911.

Born in Waterford, Michigan, in 1868, Gates graduated from the College of Mines at the University of Michigan with a degree in mining engineering. It wasn't until after the turn of the century that he came west and settled in Denver, where he married Hazel Rhoads and started the Colorado Tire and Leather Company. The product manufactured was called "Durable Tread," a steel-studded band of elkhide which fastened over the flimsy tires of automobiles to give them greater road life.

The company was later renamed the International Tire Company when it began the production of tires, and then became Gates Rubber, a name which became familiar throughout the nation.

The manufacture of belts for power-driven heavy machinery was Gates' next major venture, and by 1960 the company set up international operations.

At the age of 80, Gates was still putting in eight- to ten-hour days, managing the many facets of the operation. He died in 1961, at the age of 83.

The corporation continued to diversify, purchasing the Learjet Corporation, manufacturer of small jetcraft for large businesses, and forming a branch for maintenance of aircraft.

Gates sold the Learjet operation in 1982 to a New York firm for $63 million and bought Uniroyal's power transmission division, making Gates the leader in that industrial product, employing some 12,000 workers world-wide.

Founder of a Philanthropic Dynasty . . .

Meyer Guggenheim

The Guggenheim art museums in London, Venice, and New York; the engineering buildings on several college campuses; the Foundation for the Promotion of Aeronautics and another foundation to enable artists and scholars to study abroad: these and many more works have sprung from the efforts of a Swiss immigrant, Meyer Guggenheim.

He was born at Langnau, Switzerland, in 1828 and came to the United States in 1847. He first engaged in a business to import Swiss embroidery, but when Leadville boomed in 1879 he moved to Colorado with his family and became the main financier of the fabulous AY and Minnie mine, which brought in a hundred thousand dollars a month. With his sons Simon, William, Daniel, Murray and Solomon he maintained diverse mining interests throughout the West, including a near-monopoly in copper. The firm established a smelter at Pueblo and when the American Smelting and Refining Company (A.S. & R.) tried to crush the enterprise, son Daniel took the offensive and took over the A.S. & R.

Another son, Simon, became a U.S. senator from Colorado.

Marguerite Guggenheim, Meyer's granddaughter, was a patron of artists and modern art and endowed the various art museums in Europe and America.

Meyer Guggenheim died in 1905, leaving a legacy famous throughout the world.

Cattle King of the Plains . . .

John Wesley Iliff

Colorado's most famous rancher, who became the ideal representative of the Western livestock industry nationwide, amassed millions of dollars without resorting to the bullying of homesteaders which characterized some other cattle barons.

The son of a stock raiser, John Wesley Iliff was born near Zanesville, Ohio, in 1831 and studied at Ohio Wesleyan College. Although named for the founder of Methodism and reared as a Methodist, he never joined a church. After learning stock breeding on the family farm, he went to Kansas in 1856 and started a store with a $500 gift from his father. Before long he founded the town of Ohio City (now known as Princeton). When gold fever hit Colorado in 1859, he moved to Denver to sell groceries and clothes, often taking as payment wagon train oxen and mules emaciated after the long trek across the plains. Iliff nursed the lean animals back to health and sold them for a substantial profit in the mining camps. Soon he was branching into cattle, buying Texas longhorns brought north along the Goodnight-Loving Trail. He imported breeding stock from Illinois and Iowa to improve the strain and found himself buying plots of land along the South Platte River to the Nebraska border for grazing.

Iliff ran as many as 26,000 head at a time, with nine separate camps. He employed only cowboys of good character and forbade the use of alcohol. Rather than remaining an aloof executive, he often rode with his men. One lament he felt was that the West needed more ministers to raise moral standards.

Sarah Smith of Kansas became his wife in 1864, but she died giving birth to their son, William, the next year. He later married Elizabeth Fuller and moved to Cheyenne for a few years before returning to Denver, where John Wesley Iliff died in 1878 at the age of 46, leaving an estate of $5,000,000. Elizabeth donated $100,000 for the formation of Iliff Seminary, which would later be affiliated with the University of Denver, for the training of ministers to serve the West.

Through the years, with careful and efficient management of the cattle empire, she and William doubled the value of the estate.

Merchant Prince of the West . . .
David May

When he arrived in Leadville, David May tried his hand at mining but soon realized that the boom town of 30,000 needed long red woolen underwear and Levis. He opened a store in a tent-like structure and prospered, later taking on a partner, Elias Schonberg, whose sister he fell in love with and later married. The clothing business grew into one of the nation's leading department store chains, The May Company.

Born near Frankfurt, Germany, in 1848, May came to the United States at an early age and secured a job in Hartford City, Indiana. It was then that he contracted the scourge of the nineteenth century, tuberculosis, and, in 1877 moved to Manitou Springs to "take the cure." Soon after that, the silver boom at Leadville began, and he moved to the "Cloud City" to seek his fortune. The venture there soon led to branch stores at Pueblo, Irwin, Glenwood Springs, and Aspen. In 1885, May bought out his partner and the firm became known simply as The May Company. Three years later, he purchased a bankrupt store in Denver and, with a brass band to advertise its opening, sold the entire stock within days. Thus was established the pilot operation which spread soon to St. Louis, Cleveland, Akron, and Los Angeles.

May also had a political career, serving as the Lake County treasurer. He declined to run for the state treasurer's post, although sought for that service, due to the expansion of his business interests. At the end of the century, he refused the post of consul at Frankfurt, Germany, offered to him by President McKinley.

May was a philanthropist, giving generously to Temple Emanuel and National Jewish Hospital. When stricken with a heart attack, he went to Charlevoix, Michigan, to recuperate—

ironically–in the lower altitude. He died there in 1927 at the age of 79.

The Union Leaders

Founder of an International Labor Union . . .

William Dudley "Big Bill" Haywood

One of the most rambunctious organizers in the turbulent days of early labor unions was "Big Bill" Haywood, who founded the Industrial Workers of the World (IWW) to oppose the American Federation of Labor. His career was riddled with accusations of advocating violence in the labor strikes, but he helped to bring to the attention of the world the deplorable conditions in which working men were exploited and driven to their deaths through poor safety and health practices.

Bill Haywood was born in Salt Lake City in 1869. His father died when he was only four years of age, but his mother remarried, and they moved to mining camps in Utah and Nevada, exposed to violence of every type. Becoming involved with the Western Federation of Miners while working as a miner at Silver City, Idaho, he soon rose to a position of leadership. He was married to Nevada Jane Minor, and they moved to Denver in 1901, where he was secretary-treasurer of the nationwide mining union.

One account suggests that his method of keeping records consisted of making notes on scraps of papers and old envelopes and tucking them under his derby hat.

He joined the Socialist Party and worked his way up to membership in the executive committee.

Haywood was arrested and tried in Idaho as an accomplice to the murder of Governor Frank Steunenberg, a deed accomplished by notorious dynamiter Harry Orchard. With famed trial lawyer Clarence Darrow as his defender, he was acquitted. In 1917, however, when the United States entered World War I, Haywood, a suspected threat to national security, was sentenced to serve out the war in Leavenworth prison. Obtaining release on bail, he fled to the new Soviet

Union, where he was hailed as an escapee from capitalism, and remained there until his death in 1928.

His alleged autobiography, *Bill Haywood's Book*, was published the following year but is believed to have been ghost-written by a Soviet author.

Buccaneer of Land Reform . . .

James George Patton

Out in Western Colorado is the town of Nucla, founded as a utopian cooperative farm settlement dedicated to equality and service rather than greed and competition. Its idealistic beginnings have long since dissolved, but its basic philosophy permeated American agricultural policy and even influenced world food production. James Patton, born in Kansas in 1902, grew up in Nucla, firmly dedicated to the humanitarian view of farming.

After high school in Grand Junction, he studied at Western State College, Gunnison, to which he attributed his leadership ability. He was one of the nation's most influential forces in agriculture for three decades, during the presidencies of F.D. Roosevelt, Truman, Eisenhower, Kennedy, and Johnson. Much of it was in an adversarial role; he was president of the National Farmers Union from 1940 until his retirement in 1966, re-elected unanimously fifteen times.

Patton started out as a teacher and married Velma Fouse when he was instructing at Eckert. Later, in Denver, he established an insurance program for depression-ridden farmers and soon rose to the leadership of the Colorado Farmers Union. By the end of the Thirties, he was elected to head the national organization and, from that time on, no President would act on agricultural policies without consulting the leader of a million farmers. He also served as an adviser to the National Youth Administration, launched a world food program, and promoted rural electrification.

He lost his left eye to cancer and wore an eye patch which prompted journalists to give him the monicker, "Buccaneer of the Land."

Patton retired in 1966, and the United World Federalists elected him to their presidency. Still in the center of controversy, he died in 1986 in Washington, D.C.

The Lawyers

First Woman Lawyer . . .

Mary Florence Lathrop

When she argued a case regarding the will of Denver's George W. Clayton, in which he bequeathed funds to start an orphanage, Mary Lathrop took on the powerful firm which was representing Clayton's descendants and seeking to perpetuate the Colorado custom of disallowing such donations. She traced common law all the way back to the Louisiana Purchase and won the case, allowing the orphanage to become a reality. At the same time, she reorganized Colorado's probate system.

Mary Lathrop was the first woman in the nation to be admitted to the American Bar Association, as well as to the Denver and Colorado Bar. A native of Philadelphia, she was born in 1865. She worked for a newspaper there, but then was hired by the McClure magazines to become a correspondent in the West. She traveled by stagecoach to cover Indian wars, racial strife on the West Coast, and other events of the Eighties. She contracted pneumonia and then tuberculosis, prompting her move to Denver for recovery. It was then that she decided to break into that great male bastion, the legal profession.

Lathrop studied at the University of Denver and was admitted to legal practice upon her graduation in 1896. She specialized in probate and real estate but refused to take divorce cases.

During World War I, she sold Liberty Bonds and gave speeches promoting their sale. In World War II, she hosted enlisted men at dinners in Denver and held special holiday parties for the GIs. In all, she entertained more than 14,000 soldiers. Mary Florence Lathrop died in 1951.

Founder of the Juvenile Court System...

Benjamin Barr Lindsey

As a young man, Ben Lindsey worked in a law office in Denver. His father had died, the family had not made the last payment on his life insurance, and they were reduced to abject poverty. Ben worked so hard and long, denying himself adequate food to pay the costs of his books as he studied law, that one night he became desperate. Placing a loaded revolver to his head, he pulled the trigger. By some miracle, the cartridge failed to explode. Lindsey took a whole new look at life. A decade later, Judge Lindsey established a model juvenile court system which made a difference to the future of thousands of the nation's delinquents, as judicial strategy gradually shifted from punishment to rehabilitation.

Ben was born in Jackson, Tennessee, in 1869. The family moved to Denver in 1880, where his father was a telegraph operator. Young Ben was sent back to Indiana to attend school and then returned to Denver, where he inherited the awesome responsibilities attending his father's demise. With the amazing failure of his suicide, he continued to study and passed the bar examination in 1894, a time when Denver's civic corruption was at its worst. However, he gradually worked his way up in a respectable law practice and in 1900 was elected county judge on a reform platform.

In those days, juvenile offenders were placed in the same cells as hardened criminals and often learned a criminal's view of the law. Lindsey realized this was not the right attitude for rehabilitation, and he began giving out more sentences of probation with stern lectures and follow-up, a procedure he followed when young **Gene Fowler** and **Paul Whiteman** were brought before him for greasing the tracks of a trolley. Lindsey gave delinquents carfare to Golden, where they reported on their own to the reformatory. Very few skipped their duties after his kindly admonitions. In 1903, he established a juvenile court which became a model for the nation. In the meantime, his continuous fights with the establishment made him the center of controversy. In 1910, he wrote a book, *The Beast*, exposing some of the graft and deception of the system. By 1914, Ben Lindsey was named in a national poll one of the ten greatest living Americans.

Lindsey had other controversial ideas, including trial marriage and sex education, which brought him under constant attack. During the Ku Klux Klan era, he was the target of sophisticated efforts to disbar him and, when things got too tense in the Capitol, he would retreat to his ranch near Paonia. In 1928, he was ousted from law practice in a rigged case. Although fully reinstated, he moved to California, where he continued to practice law until his death in 1943.

From Rhodes Scholar to the Highest Court . . .

Byron R. White

Neither a liberal nor a conservative, Byron White's opinions as a Supreme Court justice have frequently been decisive ones in American law.

Born in 1917 in Fort Collins, he attended schools in Wellington, where he graduated, continuing on to the University of Colorado. There he maintained a straight 'A' average and took part in football, basketball, and baseball. His prowess on the gridiron prompted a Denver sportswriter to hang the moniker "Whizzer" on him, a nickname he loathes. He was an All-American, leading the C.U. Buffaloes to the Cotton Bowl in 1939.

Winning the coveted Rhodes Scholarship, White asked for a deferment to play football for the Pittsburgh Steelers. He went to Oxford University, attaining honors there and then enrolling at Yale University to attend law school. He played two seasons with the Detroit Lions before enlisting in the Navy during World War II. Among the men he came to know in the service was John F. Kennedy, later President of the United States. After his Naval stint he returned to Yale, graduating with honors in 1946, after which he took a position as law clerk for Chief Justice Fred M. Vinson of the Supreme Court. He later practiced law in Denver.

Kennedy appointed him to the high court in 1962, and he has garnered an international reputation for his interpretations on important decisions, including those on birth control restrictions, racial equality, and limitation of military surveillance of civilians. He is married and the father of two, a son and a daughter.

The Political Leaders

Secretary of Agriculture . . .

Charles F. Brannan

A staunch New Deal Democrat, Charles Franklin Brannan was a native Denverite, born in 1903. He received his law degrees from the University of Denver. In 1948, President Truman named him U.S. Secretary of Agriculture.

Brannan married Edna Seltzer in 1932, when he was practicing law in Denver. Beginning in 1935, he was to occupy a number of positions with the U.S. Department of Agriculture, moving up to the post of assistant secretary in 1944. During World War II, he was a key decision-maker in the program which provided food for America's allies from England and the Mediterranean to India and China.

During his tenure of office as secretary, Brannan was noted for the institution of farm programs recommended by Farmers' Union president **James Patton**, and many of those principles are still extant in U.S. farm policy. He resigned from the office with the election of Eisenhower and returned to private practice.

"Smilingest" Secretary of Interior . . .

Oscar Chapman

A liberal Democrat throughout his professional career, Oscar Chapman was branded a leftist by his critics but held to the moderate "New Deal" position, credited by some historians as staving off the threat of Communism in the days of the Great Depression. He was also termed the "smilingest" man in public office and was known as the easiest to see in Washington, D.C.

Chapman was born in 1896 in Omega, Virginia, and graduated from the Randolph-Macon Academy in Bedford, Virginia, just in time to join the U.S. Navy in World War I, serving as a pharmacist's mate. He made 36 crossings of the Atlantic during the war.

Contracting tuberculosis after the war, he moved to Denver for the high, dry climate. There he became assistant chief probation officer for famous juvenile court Judge **Ben Lindsey**. At the same time, he studied at the University of Denver and later took a leave to study at the University of New Mexico. Chapman returned to Denver to become chief probation officer and finished his law degree at Westminster Law School. He became the junior law partner of reforming Senator Edward Costigan in 1929.

With Franklin D. Roosevelt's victory in 1932, Chapman became the Assistant Secretary of Interior, serving under the "Old Curmudgeon," Harold Ickes. His more democratic methods did not go over well with Ickes, so promotions were few.

It wasn't until Ickes stepped down in 1946 that Chapman was elevated to the position of Undersecretary of the Interior. In 1949, he was made Secretary of the Interior, holding office until the advent of the Eisenhower administration in 1953. During that period, he made a number of important decisions regarding National Park conservation and the rehabilitation of America's overseas possessions, always inviting those involved to come and talk over their concerns with him.

In 1953, he retired from government service to become a partner in a Washington law firm. He died in 1978 at the age of 81.

Doctor Who Founded Universities . . .

John Evans

John Evans was a founder of many institutions in the Midwest and in Denver; he was a governor and a senator; he started two railroads and edited a medical journal; he was also an inventor of medical equipment and a noted teacher.

Born a Quaker on a farm two miles from Wanesville, Ohio, in 1814, he was educated in the Friends School there and later at the Friends Academy in Richmond, Ohio. He attended the College of Medicine in Cincinnati, where he received his MD in 1838.

He first practiced in Ohio and Indiana. At Indianapolis, he was instrumental in founding the first hospital for the insane and became its first superintendent. Evans then moved to Chicago, where he had a private practice as well as being a member of the Rush Medical College. It was there that he invented an obstetrical extractor.

He then became interested in real estate investments and in the publication and editorship of the *Northwestern Medical and Surgical Journal*. He helped establish Mercy Hospital in Chicago and developed the land which became Evanston, Illinois, nearby. Converting to Methodism, he was instrumental in the founding of Garrett Biblical Institute and Northwestern University, both in Evanston. He also served on the Chicago City Council and was among the first delegates to what became the Illinois Republican Party.

Relinquishing his medical practice in 1857, Evans promoted a railroad from Chicago to Omaha and then land developments in Nebraska. He was an outspoken opponent of slavery and a supporter of Lincoln, who appointed him governor of the Colorado Territory in 1862. Moving to Denver, he helped establish the Colorado Seminary, which eventually became the University of Denver. After the tragic Sand Creek Massacre in 1864, he was removed as governor, but was appointed senator from Colorado by the Territorial Assembly a few years later.

As a leader of the Denver Board of Trade, he invested heavily in Denver real estate. He also became the motivating power behind the Denver Pacific Railroad, the Denver and South Park Railroad, and the origins of the Denver and Texas Railroad. He was a founder of a bank and held a large block of stock in Denver utilities.

In 1870 Colorado citizens renamed Mount Rosalie (named for the wife of famed painter Albert Bierstadt) to Mount Evans.

His first wife, Hannah, died in 1850, after giving birth to four children, all of whom died in infancy or childhood. He then married Margaret Gray, whose children, William and Evan, survived John when he died in 1897.

The historic Byers-Evans House, a memory of his heritage, has recently been restored by the Colorado Historical Society and is now open to the public.

Secretary of Commerce in a Stock Market Crash . . .

Robert Patterson Lamont

Robert Lamont was doomed to have to answer to the nation when the stock market crash of 1929 touched off the Great Depression. He had just been named Secretary of Commerce by President Herbert Hoover, a credit to his business and engineering career as a resident of Denver. But it was too late to turn around the conditions which brought on the collapse: critical agricultural failures, a mania for mergers, failure of small banks nationwide, unrestricted sale of stock for prices far exceeding actual asset value, and the approaching tariffs which would destroy the world market for American goods.

Born in Detroit in 1867, Lamont was trained as an engineer, graduating from the University of Michigan. He was married and the father of three children. His fame came early as engineer for the celebrated Chicago Columbian Exposition of 1893. Lamont was heavily involved in the planning and preparation of that famous world's fair, which introduced, among many other attractions, the first Ferris Wheel.

He continued his career in engineering, moving to Denver and establishing a business, gradually becoming an expert in commerce. Hoover, himself an engineer, was also impressed with Lamont's active participation in Republican Party politics. With the election of Franklin Roosevelt in 1932, Lamont returned to Denver, where he retired.

Policewoman, Industrialist, Cabinet Officer . . .

Josephine Aspinwall Roche

Voted one of the ten outstanding women in the United States in 1936, Josephine Roche was a scrappy reformer in many fields. Eleanor Roosevelt called her one of the great humanitarians of her time; her political enemies and powers like John D. Rockefeller called her, to put it politely, an insipid upstart.

Born in 1886 in Neligh, Nebraska, she moved to Denver in 1908, when her father became owner of the Rocky Mountain Fuel Company. She graduated from Vassar College and Columbia University. During World War I, she served on a committee for Belgian relief. Upon returning to Denver, she served as director of the girls' department of Judge **Ben Lindsey**'s famed juvenile court and became a key political opponent of the Denver power structure during the Progressive Era. This led to her appointment as Denver's first policewoman, patrolling the saloons and lamenting the treatment of women. A believer in women's rights, she also became angry over the treatment of children, spending some time with the U.S. Children's Agency in Washington, D.C., where she studied the relationship between poverty and juvenile delinquency. When her father died, she returned to Denver to head the fuel company and astonished competitors like Rockefeller by *inviting* union organization, raising miners' wages, and donating surface lands so that workers could have their own farms above the mines north of Denver.

The Great Depression slammed her company, and in spite of support from the miners it never did recover. Because of her humane treatment of her employees, she attracted the attention of the First Lady and then of President Franklin D. Roosevelt himself. He named her Assistant Secretary of Labor in 1934. She was only the second woman to hold even a subcabinet rank in the federal government.

Roche resigned the post in 1937 to try to save her ailing Rocky Mountain Fuel Company, but the firm did fail during

World War II. In the post-war era, she served as a director of the United Mine Workers' pension fund.

In her mid-sixties, Roche retired to Washington, D.C., still interested in being close to the national political scene. She entered a convalescent home in Bethesda, Maryland, where she died in 1976, having passed her ninetieth birthday.

Founder of the Bureau of Land Management . . .

Edward Thomas Taylor

A vehement protester against the entire concept of the national forest system in his early years, U.S. Representative Edward Taylor later favored controlled national lands so strongly that he convinced Congress to pass the Taylor Grazing Act. That landmark legislation made all grazing lands not already in the National Forest system into controlled areas, preserving them for future generations. This program was later combined with the U.S. Land Office and is now known as the Bureau of Land Management, administering vast regions for agriculture, mining, and recreation.

Taylor was born in Illinois in 1858 and moved to Kansas as a youth, graduating from Leavenworth High School. In those days, such an achievement qualified a person to teach, and he came to booming Leadville as a high school teacher. In 1882 he went to the University of Michigan to pursue a law degree, returning to Leadville as superintendent of schools. His failing health in that city, the highest in North America, forced him to move to Aspen and then to Glenwood Springs in 1887. He set up a law practice specializing in water legislation and won election to the Colorado Assembly. He was a charter member of the Colorado Bar Association and became known as the "Father of Western Water Legislation." However, he was opposed to forest regulation and confronted **William Kreutzer**, the first forest ranger, on several challenges to national law. With the turn of the century, though, he changed his politics from Republican to Democrat and was elected to the U.S. House of Representatives in 1909, a position he held for 32 years. He also authored more statutes than any other congressman of his era. Gradually he accepted and then promoted the multiple-use concept of the Forest Service.

By 1931, he was pushing for the extension of multiple use and restriction of homesteading on the remaining lands, and in 1934 the Taylor Grazing Act became law. He convinced the Roosevelt administration to make Hayden's noted rancher-lawyer, Farrington Carpenter, the first director of the Grazing Service, leading to cooperative agreements throughout the West among cattle and sheep ranchers. In other legislation, he introduced in 1931 the bill that made "The Star Spangled Banner" the national anthem and was the author of the bill creating the dam named for him on the Taylor River near Gunnison. (The river was named for an earlier Taylor.)

Ed Taylor never lost an election and was never opposed in his own party. Married to Etta Tabor of Iowa in 1892, they had three children. In 1940, he was elected to his eleventh term in Congress even though he was unable to return to Colorado to campaign, due to the altitude. He died in Denver on the way to a speech in 1941, victim of a heart attack at the age of 83.

He Tried to Help the Indians ...

Henry M. Teller

Henry M. Teller was Colorado's first U.S. Senator and later was appointed Secretary of the Interior. He made the reform of the Indian Service his top priority and sent **Helen Hunt Jackson** to California to investigate conditions there. When he switched from the Republican to the Democratic party in 1896, his new party considered him a candidate for President of the United States.

Teller was born in 1830 in Allegheny County, New York, taught in a country school there, and hauled lumber on the Erie Canal. He worked his passage to Cincinnati and then to Paris, Kentucky, before settling in Erie, Pennsylvania, where he attended Alfred Academy. He went back to teach at Angelina and Cuba, New York, while reading for the bar, passing the exams in 1858. Teller served as an attorney in New York before moving to Denver in 1861. Soon he was a mining lawyer at Golden and in Gilpin County. His interests in investment made him a leader in the establishment of many enterprises in the new territory, including the railroad from Central City to Golden. When Colorado became a state in 1876, Teller was sent to Washington as senator until 1882, when President Chester Arthur named him Secretary of the Interior.

He fought a stubborn congress, and sometime a stubborn President, for more education for American Indians, and defended the rights of the "five civilized tribes" of Oklahoma when their land was taken away. In 1885, he returned to the Senate and became notorious to his party as a "silver Republican," one who defended silver coinage despite his party's policy.

Teller bolted the party in 1896 and threw his support to Democratic nominee William S. Bryan, but the old warhorse got himself elected to the Senate by the Democrats and served until 1909.

Teller was married, and his three children were all born at Central City. He died in 1914.

Teller County, created from El Paso County in 1899, was named for him to celebrate his work in promoting silver coinage.

Our Man in Moscow . . .

Llewelyn Thompson, Jr.

The man who served as ambassador to the Soviet Union during the height of the "Cold War" was a native of Las Animas. Llewelyn E. Thompson, Jr., was born there in 1904 and studied in the local schools. He also worked as a cowhand, in a general store, and then in a Washington lumber camp.

He met a diplomat while at work in Seattle and was inspired to enroll at the University of Colorado, where he worked his way through his undergraduate program before being accepted by Georgetown University's prestigious Foreign Service School. When he graduated in 1929, he began a career as a diplomat which spanned four decades, serving under six presidents.

He was vice consul in Ceylon (Sri Lanka) and consul at Geneva before going to the Soviet Union, where he served during World War II and again from 1958-1962, the time of the Cuban Missile Crisis. He developed a genuine friendship with Nikita Khrushchev, who was noted for his cantankerous animosity toward the United States, probably because both had rural backgrounds. When he returned to Washington, D.C., he became President Kennedy's "resident Kremlinologist."

Among his other assignments were posts in Rome and Vienna. He married Jane Goelet of Pennsylvania in 1948. When Thompson returned to America from Moscow, he received the Presidential Award for Distinguished Civilian Service, the highest honor the government can bestow upon a civilian.

Ambassador Thompson died in 1972 at the age of 67.

Cleaning Up After Teapot Dome . . .
Hubert Work

Hubert Work had the unenviable job of re-establishing some modicum of confidence in the Department of the Interior after the scandalous Teapot Dome Scandal, a notorious sale of Naval reserve oil lands to powerful private interests. He had been appointed Secretary of the Interior when Albert Fall was ousted for participation in the bribery that marked the greatest of several humiliations in the administration of President Warren Harding.

A native of Indiana County, Pennsylvania, Work was born in 1860. He worked his way through the Indiana Normal

School there and then transferred to the University of Pennsylvania, where he studied medicine, earning his MD in 1885. He set up a private practice in Greeley, serving both Greeley and Fort Lupton. Work was very interested in mental disease, so in 1896 he moved to Pueblo and founded the Woodcroft Sanatorium for Mental and Nervous Disorders. (The institution was acquired in 1923 as a unit of the Colorado State Hospital.) His prominence was such that he served as president of the American Medical Association and the American Psychiatric Association.

It was in politics, though, that he was most noted. He was state chairman of the Republican party in 1912, and, in 1928, was chosen to chair the National Republican Committee. In the meantime, he had been appointed Postmaster General in 1921, and in 1923, after the Teapot Dome Scandal, he was named Secretary of the Interior. He set up an "open door" policy, meeting with any and all reporters and other interested complainants and worked hard to see that corrupt officials in the department were fired. He was able to reduce expenditures by $129 million in three years by getting rid of excess and non-functioning positions in the organization.

Work remained at Interior throughout the Coolidge administration, leaving in 1928 for retirement in Colorado. He had been married twice. His first wife, Laura, died in 1924, and he later married Ethel Gano, who survived him when he passed away in 1942.

The Defenders

Chief of Naval Operations . . .

Arleigh Albert Burke

Arleigh Burke rose from an ensign to an admiral in charge of the entire U.S. Navy and was a negotiator in the Korean Armistice. Born in Boulder in 1901, he received an appointment to the U.S. Naval Academy after his high school graduation. Graduating from the academy in 1923, Burke later earned a Master of Science degree from the University of Michigan.

During World War II, he commanded a destroyer squadron, and was promoted to Chief of Staff of the Atlantic Fleet following the war. With the outbreak of the Korean conflict, he commanded Cruiser Division 5 and became a participant in the peace agreements.

In 1955, Burke reached the highest active role in the Navy, that of Chief of Naval Operations, and continued in that command until his retirement in 1961. Burke was the recipient of the Navy Cross and the Legion of Merit, plus many foreign citations.

After his retirement, Burke served as a director for several corporations, the Freedoms Foundation, and the national Boy Scouts of America.

First Woman Captain in the Merchant Marine . . . At 68! . . .

Mary Parker Converse

Few people have led a life as spirited as that of Mary Parker Converse. Born in Malden, Massachusetts, in 1872, she was married to wealthy heir Harry Converse in 1891. They enjoyed trips abroad, yachting, and a luxurious social life. The yacht *Parthenia* was her greatest joy, and she taught her five children the ways of seamanship. However, she separated from Harry in 1910 and dedicated herself to the writing of children's stories and songs. When World War I broke out, she joined the Red Cross and served as an entertainer for the troops.

Following the war, she became interested in prison reform in the United States and was a key influence for change in Colorado's penal program. She made Denver her home for the rest of her life, although she often wintered in California.

From 1936-1939, she shipped out four times to learn modern navigation techniques, even though she was already over 60. By 1940, Mary had successfully served all the active time required and had passed the written examinations. She was then made a captain in the U.S. Merchant Marine, the first woman so designated in the history of the service.

During World War II, she taught "V-7" training courses in Denver for men seeking merchant marine commissions, often at her home on High Street, which was also a leading attraction for the social set. She was accepted for membership in the British Institute of Navigation, another first for a woman. This led to interviews on national radio networks, and, in 1952, *Navigation* magazine dedicated an entire issue to her career.

Her book *Kiddie Pals* was published when she was over 50, and at the age of 67 she published the musical composition, "Sextet for Strings and Woodwinds."

Then in her eighties, Captain Mary helped raise funds for the Denver Civic Symphony and worked to promote **Walter Orr Roberts'** High Altitude Observatory at Boulder and Climax. She found time to write another book, *On Becoming a Mariner*, and also gave lectures. The Mary Parker Converse Seminar Room at the University of Colorado Astrophysics Building was named in her honor.

Captain Mary died in 1961.

The First Draftee to Become a Four-Star General ...

Robert E. "Dutch" Huyser

Dutch Huyser had barely graduated from Paonia High School when his draft notice arrived in 1942. Born near Paonia in 1924, he had compiled a fine record as a student and qualified as an aviation cadet in the Army Air Corps, soon flying B-24s and B-29s on combat missions and commissioned a "shavetail" second lieutenant.

From then on his career moved into high gear as he demonstrated outstanding leadership talent. He was chief of combat operations for the Far East Bomber Command in the Korean Conflict. As the Air Force became a separate branch, he was a recognized leader in jet aviation. By 1969, Dutch was promoted to Brigadier General and was Chief of Command Control at the Strategic Air Command. His work in developing strategic nuclear war plans for all U.S. forces brought another promotion, and he was moved into the Pentagon as director of plans and operations for the Air Force.

By 1975, Robert Huyser was made a four-star general, the highest rank which can be attained during peacetime and the first draftee in American history to have reached that rank. With it came assignment as commander-in-chief of the U.S. European Command, and later commander-in-chief of the Military Airlift Command.

He was then sent on a special mission to Iran to investigate the collapse of the Shah's regime to the Ayatollah Khomeini, the capture of the U.S. Embassy in Tehran, and the ensuing hostage crisis. His book on that subject, *Mission to Tehran*, is one of the most significant explanations of the entire tragic affair.

Huyser officially retired in 1981 but continued to work with youth groups, as a lecturer throughout the nation, and as a consultant for the Boeing Corporation.

Marine Corps Commandant . . .

Lewis W. Walt

A much decorated Marine from Fort Collins rose to the highest position in that branch of the U.S. Armed Forces.

Lewis Walt was born in 1913 and studied chemistry at Colorado State University (then Colorado A. and M. College), graduating in 1936. He joined the service and became a second lieutenant in the Marine Corps.

During World War II, Walt was awarded the Navy Cross two times. In the Korean Conflict, he won the Legion of Honor. He became a general in the Vietnam War and was promoted to lieutenant general in 1966.

In 1969, Lewis Walt was named a four-star general and was made commandant of the U.S. Marine Corps, retiring a decade later.

He married Nancy Sheehan, and they had three children.

The Spacemen

The Kindergartner Who Went on into Outer Space . . .

Vance Devoe Brand

Ever think of travel allowances for space travelers? Vance Brand filed a travel claim for "$25 and some cents" after a Columbia space shuttle mission. Born in Longmont in 1931, Vance was thrilled when his father took him for a ride in a Ford trimotor plane during his kindergarten days, allowing him to see how the world looked from the air. Flying became an obsession. After graduating from Longmont High School, he went on to the University of Colorado, where he took degrees in business and aeronautical engineering. He picked up a master of business administration degree at the University of California at Los Angeles in 1963 and went to work for Lockheed Aircraft as a test pilot.

Serving four years as a Marine jet fighter pilot during the Vietnam War, Vance joined the National Aeronatics and Space Administration (NASA) and was trained as an astronaut. He commanded three space flights. Perhaps the most challenging was the Apollo-Soyuz flight in 1975, when American and Soviet spacecraft docked together, opening a new era in space exploration and in relations between the two nations. In 1982, he commanded the fifth flight of the shuttle Columbia, and in 1984 he was commander of a mission of the shuttle Challenger.

He received the Distinguished Service Medal from NASA and is one of the nation's most respected astronauts today. In evaluating the shuttle program, he has maintained that "the shuttle will eventually pay for itself."

From Ensign to Astronaut to Environmentalist . . .

Malcolm Scott Carpenter

Early in the U.S. space program, Scott Carpenter took part in the three-orbit mission Aurora-7 and was able to behold the earth from a splendid viewpoint. The intensity of this experience strongly influenced him toward environmentalism, and he later became a fellow of the Institute of Environmental Scientists.

Born in Boulder in 1925, he studied aeronautical engineering at the University of Colorado. In 1949, he became an ensign in the U.S. Navy and served on active duty during the Korean War. By 1954, he was a test pilot for the Navy and by 1959 had become a commander.

The National Aeronautics and Space Administration chose Carpenter as one of the first to work on outer space endeavors, signing him for the Project Mercury "Man in Space" project in 1959. In May of 1962, he was a member of the Aurora-7 mission.

Moving to Houston after his retirement from NASA, he entered private business and maintained his interest in preserving the planet he viewed from space. Later he worked in Los Angeles with oceanographic research.

The Man on the Moon . . .

Stuart Roosa

Pilot of Command Module XIV, which landed on the moon in 1971, Stuart Roosa is one of the few people ever to view the earth from its greatest satellite.

Roosa was born in Durango in 1933 and attended schools there before going to Oklahoma State and then the University of Arizona, where he obtained a BS degree in aeronautical engineering.

A command officer in the United States Air Force by 1953, he became a crack test pilot at Edwards Air Force Base in California.

His experience in space included being a member of the support crew of Apollo IX, and he was awarded NASA's Distinguished Service Medal before his retirement from the Air Force.

Roosa later became president of Gulf Coast Coors, Inc., at Gulfport, Mississippi. He married Joan Barrett, and they had four children.

A Tense Moment in Outer Space . . .

John Leonard Swigert, Jr.

Looping around the moon in April of 1970, astronaut John Swigert's crew on Apollo XIII discovered a fuel-cell rupture in the oxygen tank of their service module. After almost 143 hours in space, the third manned trip to the moon was aborted, and creative use of the lunar landing module enabled the crew to return safely to the earth.

Swigert was born in 1931 in Denver and studied at the University of Colorado, Rensselaer Polytechnic Institute, and the University of Hartford. He joined the Air Force in 1953, serving as a fighter pilot assigned to Korea. He was later a test pilot for Pratt-Whitney and North American Aviation before entering the NASA astronaut program in 1966. Swigert was awarded a medal from the American Institute of Aeronautics and Astronautics for demonstrating the Rogallo Wing, a feasible landing system for returning space vehicles.

For his dangerous and heroic work in the Apollo 13 flight, he was presented with the Medal of Freedom in 1970.

The subject of dramatic stories in several periodicals, he was also author of a number of tracts on space technology. His hobbies included sports and photography.

Although suffering from cancer in 1982, John Swigert was a successful candidate for the U.S. House of Representatives from Arapahoe and Jefferson counties but died on December 28, 1982, just seven days before he was to be sworn into office.

The Athletes

The Manassa Mauler . . .
William Harrison (Jack) Dempsey

He has been called Colorado's greatest all-time professional athlete. In 1919, at Toledo, Ohio, Jack Dempsey knocked out Jess Willard in the third round, becoming the world's heavyweight boxing champion. He retained the championship until he lost a ten-round decision to Gene Tunney in 1926, and was regarded as a national hero for the rest of his life.

Dempsey was born in 1895 in the little San Luis Valley town of Manassa and spent his youth living in different communities, including Delta, Montrose and Cripple Creek. He started boxing at Montrose and then went on to bigger matches at Cripple Creek, using the name "Kid Blackie." As his fame spread and he won at Salt Lake City, Dempsey took on the big-time boxers. A sportswriter called him "the Manassa Mauler," and it became a widely used moniker.

He retired from the ring in 1940, having saved enough for a broad range of investments. He was most noted for the restaurant he opened in New York City, a haven for sports lovers from all over the world. *Round by Round*, his autobiography, was published on his retirement.

Jack Dempsey died in 1983, an athlete who will always be remembered as one of Colorado's famous native sons.

Poetic Basketball Star . . .
Alexander English

Born in Columbia, South Carolina, in 1954, Alex English was educated at the University of South Carolina and, after graduation, became a forward for the Milwaukee Bucks basketball team. After two years, he joined the Indiana Pacers and in 1980 came to Denver as a Denver Nugget.

English reached the peak of his career as a Nugget. He was the leading scorer of the National Basketball Association (NBA) and was selected for NBA All-Star games

As an avocation he has written poetry, and he is noted for his generous support of charitable causes.

Master Mountaineer . . .
Layton Kor

Colorado has produced numerous outstanding mountain climbers, including such men as Carl Blaurock, Robert Ormes, Dwight Lavender, and Albert Ellingwood. One who attained international fame for his skill in climbing vertical rock faces was Layton Kor, who made a hundred "first ascents" in little more than a decade, scaling peaks in the West, Canada, Alaska, and the Alps.

Kor was a youth in Colorado Springs in the early 1950s when he saw the television movie "Man Against the Matterhorn." Taking his father's geology pick, he tried his first ascent, climbing a nearby clay formation, and began to learn what doesn't work. When the family moved to Texas, he had to settle for scaling trees with pitons and ropes, but finally they resettled in Boulder, where he could develop his forte. A strapping 200-pounder, standing 6 feet 5 inches, he could climb with more speed and skill than many others of the Sixties generation, helping rekindle mountaineering fever in Colorado.

Among his achievements in Colorado were the first winter ascent of the formidable Diamond on the East Face of Longs Peak and the first ascents of the highest vertical face in the state, the wall of the Black Canyon of the Gunnison. Abroad, he led the first winter ascent of Switzerland's Eiger and the North Face of Cima Ouest in the Italian Alps. He was acclaimed by all his climbing partners, and *National Geographic Magazine* featured his dangerous climb in the Fisher Towers of Utah. A stonemason by trade, Kor was said to have the strongest set of hands in climbing.

His excitement for the sport diminished late in the Sixties, especially after the tragic death of one of his partners on a Swiss climb. He married and settled down to raise a family, relegating his climbing career to the back-burner and giving more attention to the religious interests he had discovered.

World's Featherweight Boxing Champ . . .
William Rothwell (Young Corbett)

When he beat "Terrible Terry" McGovern in a second-round knockout in 1901 at Hartford, Connecticut, "Young Corbett" amazed the boxing world. And when he voluntarily relinquished the title by "failing to make weight" so that others could have a go at the world featherweight championship, he became a hero of the first magnitude.

William Rothwell was born in Denver in 1880 and had his first boxing matches there in 1897. His phenomenal fist power rocketed him to the top within four years. He adopted the name "Young Corbett" after his manager, Johnny Corbett. In the year following his triumph, he felt he had achieved all he wanted and abandoned the title, allowing Abe Attell to replace him. He kept on boxing, though, and did not retire from the ring until 1910. Rothwell stayed in New York until 1921, when he moved back to his home city. He was only 46 when his heart collapsed as he crossed a downtown Denver street in 1927.

First American to Take a European Ski Prize . . .

Wallace "Buddy" Werner

His name has been immortalized in a national skiing program for youth and by a mountain named in his memory. While Colorado has had many great national leaders in the field of skiing, Buddy Werner's name is known across the nation.

Ed and Hazel Werner raised a family of skiers: Skeeter, Buddy, and Loris, all of whom made names for themselves on the slopes. Buddy was born at Steamboat Springs, Colorado's consummate ski pioneering center, in 1936. At Steamboat High, he was coached by Al Wegeman and Gordon Wren, both members of the Colorado Ski Hall of Fame.

Buddy became the first American to win a major European ski event, Austria's Hahnenhamm, in 1962. He was already a national champion, winning titles in collegiate skiing with the University of Denver's famous coach, Willy Schaeffler. He also won the Gran Prix at Chamonix, the Holemkollen, Lauberhorn, Criterium of the First Snow, Roch Cup, and the Harriman Cup.

His congenial nature was legendary among world sports figures, and he was widely recognized for the promotion of international understanding in the ski world. Recipient of the National Ski Hall of Fame Athlete of the Year Award, he was especially interested in helping children get started in the sport.

Werner's life was snuffed out in an avalanche in Switzerland on April 12, 1964. The Buddy Werner ski program, a nationwide instructional function for young skiers, has spread to almost all major U.S. ski areas.

America's Greatest Woman Athlete ...

Mildred "Babe" Didrickson Zaharias

In 1947 Babe Didrickson Zaharias became the first American woman to win the famous British Open golf tournament. However, that was just one more accomplishment for this lady, labeled in the *Official Encyclopedia of Sports* as "America's greatest woman athlete."

Born at Port Arthur, Texas, in 1914, Babe was already winning major sports events in high school: she was national women's high school track champion and basketball champion. She served on the All-American basketball team from 1930 to 1932 and in those same years won eight events and tied for a ninth in the national track and field championships. She won gold medals at the 1932 Los Angeles Olympic games in the 80-meter hurdles and the javelin throw. She would have won the high jump (and established a new world record) had her "Western roll" not been disqualified.

She married George Zaharias in 1938 and later moved to Denver. There she took up golf, winning the 1946 National Women's amateur title and 17 other amateur tournaments in a row, including the British Open.

After that, the Babe went professional and took first place in the U.S. Open in 1948, 1950, and 1954. She was the leading money winner on the Women's Golf Tour from 1948 to 1951.

Even after she was stricken with cancer, Babe Zaharias continued to win golf tournaments. She died in 1956 in Denver.

The Holiday Maker

Founder of Columbus Day . . .

Angelo Noce

A Denver printer was the promoter of Columbus Day as a national holiday. Born in Genoa, Italy, in 1848, Noce came to America with his family as a youth, received his education in San Francisco, and later established a printing business in Denver. At various times in his career, he was also a deputy sheriff and clerk of the Colorado Assembly, where he began pushing for the recognition of Columbus' discovery of the New World.

The additional publicity generated by Chicago's famous 1893 "Columbian Exposition," enabled Noce to convince Colorado legislators to make October 12 a holiday starting in 1907; Colorado was the first state to declare Columbus Day an official holiday. From that time on, he traveled to other states to lobby for its establishment, and by the time of his death in 1922, thirty-five states had established the holiday. In 1967 the U.S. Congress made it a national holiday.

The Record Keepers

Scholar of Western American History . . .

Robert G. Athearn

When Robert Athearn died in 1983, his former graduate students from the University of Colorado were moved to honor him with a memorial book of their essays on Western history. He was instrumental in giving a start to numerous serious historians and wrote a multitude of original studies in the form of books, articles and reviews.

Born at Kremlin, Montana, in 1914, he earned BA, MA, and PhD degrees at the University of Minnesota. He took a position on the University of Colorado faculty in 1947, and remained there for the rest of his career.

Athearn was noted as an outstanding book reviewer as well as a no-nonsense scholar. Except for service with the Coast Guard during World War II, his whole life was devoted to historical research.

In 1953 he wrote *Westward the Briton*, the first significant full-length study of the role the British played in the settlement and development of the West. He also wrote *Centennial Colorado*, *High Country Empire*, *Rebel of the Rockies*, a history of the Denver and Rio Grande Railroad, *America Moves West*, and *The Coloradans*. He edited the 16-volume *American Heritage New Illustrated History of the United States* and seven other major works, plus numerous scholarly articles.

Giving Honest History Flesh and Blood . . .

David Lavender

There is no such thing as dull history. There may be dull historians, dull history teachers, and dull history students, but the nuts and bolts of history are the recorded impressions of people who lived and died and wrote down only what they saw as exciting events in their lives. Few historians have been so conscious of this and as eloquent in the careful reconstruction of the past as David Lavender, who was born in Telluride and worked in mines and on cattle ranches, feeling experiences rather than just imagining them.

Lavender was born in 1910, and was fortunate enough after his hard-working youth to graduate from Princeton University and do graduate study at Stanford. His writing career, which has spanned more than half a century, has been supplemented by teaching at Thatcher School in Ojai, California. He stayed on in that area as a consultant to the library of the University of California at Santa Barbara.

His *Bent's Fort*, which won the Spur Award of the Western Writers of America, has been called the "most readable account of Western U.S. History ever written." An easy style makes his works, which are meticulous in historical accuracy, more enjoyable reading than many novels, demonstrating that what really happened is often more exciting than what novelists can imagine. In *One Man's West*, Lavender gave an account of his early life, with insight into how he could, by experience, really live the lives of those long gone. Among the other great works he has produced are *The Big Divide, Fist in the Wilderness, The Rockies, Colorado River Country, Climax at Buena Vista,* and *The Way to the Western Sea*. He has written pamphlets for the National Park Service and articles for *Encyclopedia Britannica*.

Lavender also wrote novels, including *Red Mountain*, and children's literature.

Historian Who Inspired the "Little Britches" Rodeos . . .

Ralph Owen Moody

Ralph Moody was only eight years old when his family moved to the upper Bear Creek Valley above Denver. His father, a New Hampshire wool mill worker, had contracted a lung disease and came west to seek a healthier atmosphere. The shack in which the Moodys started ranching was beset by wild coyotes every night. Young Ralph loved it, loved cowboys, loved the romance of the wild West. He took great delight in the youthful rodeo matches held in Littleton, where the family moved after his father died.

Ralph was born in Rochester, New Hampshire, in 1898. After his schooling in Littleton, he went on to history studies in college and married Lucille Hudgens. They had four children.

Among his outstanding historical works were *The Dry Divide, Wells Fargo, Old Trails West* (he retraced them in person), and the classic on the topic, inspired by personal acquaintance with some of the stagecoach men of his youth, *Stage Coach West.*

His autobiographical works, though, probably carried the greatest impact on the nation: *Little Britches, Man of the Family,* and *Shaking the Nickle Bush.* Littleton became noted for its youth rodeos and established the Little Britches Rodeo as an annual event. Soon, towns and cities all over the nation began to stage Little Britches rodeos. The oldest continuous such rodeo in Colorado is the one at the little town of Cedaredge.

Eventually the rodeos took on a nation-wide organization, with district, state, and national competition. For years, the national finals have been held at Colorado Springs, but, starting in 1990, they will be held in the Roundup Club Arena at Delta, a town similar to the Littleton of Moody's youth.

As his writing career progressed, the Moodys moved to Burlingame, California.

Chronicler of the Rockies . . .

Marshall Sprague

A recorder of such diverse events in the Rockies as the so-called Meeker Massacre on the Western Slope to the urbane tradition of Colorado Springs (sometimes called "Little London") at the foot of Pikes Peak, Marshall Sprague produced many books introducing the history of the region to the nation. He came to Colorado Springs as a victim of tuberculosis in 1941.

Sprague was born in Newark, Ohio, in 1909 and graduated from Lawrenceville School and Princeton University. He wrote for *Women's Wear Daily* and then became a reporter for the *North China Star* in Tientsin. His next post was with the Paris edition of the *New York Herald-Tribune*. In 1936, he returned to America as a feature writer for the *New York Times*. A married man with three children, the apparent tragedy of the dread tuberculosis came as a shock.

His gradual recovery prompted him to write *The Business of Getting Well* in 1943, and he then turned his attention to the history of Colorado.

Among his works are *Massacre: The Tragedy at White River*, a detailed account of the Ute uprising which ended in the death of Indian Agent Nathan C. Meeker and seven other men, resulting in the removal of the tribe from its giant reservation in western Colorado. Other books include *Money Mountain: The Story of Cripple Creek; This is Central City; Great Pioneer Heroes; Newport in the Rockies* (about Colorado Springs); *A Gallery of Dudes; The Great Gates;* and *Colorado: Bicentennial History*, published in 1976.

When asked about the talent for graphic historical writing, he replied, "You learn to write by writing."

A Premier Writer of Western History . . .

Agnes Wright Spring

Her career embraced a wide variety of studies and achievements. Agnes Wright Spring was born in Delta in 1894, and she attended schools there until her family moved to a ranch near Laramie, Wyoming, where her father established a stage line and freighting business between Laramie and several Wyoming mines. At the University of Wyoming, she became the first editor of the student newspaper and was the first woman to enter the engineering school. There she received the nickname "Old Ironsides" when the metal staves in her corset disturbed the compass needle used in surveying!

Agnes graduated as a civil engineer in 1913, but took a job in the library of the Wyoming Supreme Court until awarded a scholarship to Columbia University's Pulitzer School of Journalism. There she became excited about the women's suffrage movement, working with famed leaders Carrie Chapman Catt and Susan B. Anthony. Her roots were in Wyoming, the first state to allow women to vote; she rose up in indignation when offered a reporter's job in New York for half the amount of pay given to men. Instead, she returned to Wyoming, where she became the State Historian.

She married Archer Spring, a geologist, in 1921 and spent several years traveling the West with him, interviewing old-timers. They bought a cherry orchard in Fort Collins a few years later, and it was there that she wrote her first history, *Caspar Collins: The Life and Exploits of an Indian Fighter of the Sixties*. This was followed by about 20 other books, more than 600 articles and fiction stories, and a play. She also edited the *Wyoming Stockman-Farmer* for more than a quarter of a century.

During World War II, she became the Colorado State Historian, the only person to have served in such a position for more than one state. Spring achieved national recognition for both her writing and her outstanding service in development of the state historical resources, receiving honors from both the National Cowboy Hall of Fame and the National Cowgirl Hall of Fame.

At her death in 1988, she was working on a book recounting her efforts to promote women's rights in America.

Writer of Epics of the Old West . . .
Frank Joseph Waters

His books have been translated into French, Dutch, Swedish, Japanese, and German. Some critics consider him the most famous of all those who write about the Rocky Mountain region.

Born in Colorado Springs in 1902, Frank Waters attended schools there before enrolling at Colorado College, where he graduated in 1925 and began his writing career.

As a novelist, he wrote eleven volumes, including *The Man Who Killed the Deer, Pike's Peak: A Family Saga,* and *The Woman of Otowi Crossing.* He also wrote twelve nonfiction works, including the fine history of Winfield Stratton and Cripple Creek, *Midas of the Rockies.* His monumental *The Colorado* ties together the threads of the history of the Colorado River from its source to the Gulf of Lower California.

He made his home in Taos, New Mexico, becoming familiar with the lore of the Pueblo Indians and the Hispanic tradition about which he has written so much. His novel, *River Lady*, was made into a movie in 1949.

Acknowledgments and Bibliography

Acknowledgments

In a work of this type, the sources are many, by necessity. Dozens of individuals suggested names for inclusion and helped to dig out factual material not published elsewhere. Others referred the author to valuable sources of material. Space does not allow for all the singular acknowledgments the writer would prefer, but mentioned below, in alphabetical order, are some of those to whom he is greatly indebted:

David Abbott, David Batura, Robert C. Black III, Walter Borneman, Elinor Burchard, Colin Clem, Kit Collings, Maggie Coval, Wallace Dobbins, J.K. Emery, Kay Engel, David Fishell, Cara D. Fisher, Mona Gardner, Eleanor Gehres, Sharon Hill, James Holme, Sharon Kiser, Hilly Klinzmen, Jack Kelly, Phyllis Kelly, Liston Leyendecker, Shirley Lund, Donald MacKendrick, Gordon Meikeljohn, Etha Miller, Carol Moolich, Tom Noel, Phil Panum, Alan Ridgeway, Christine Steeg Scrip, Jean Sherer, Duane Smith, Elizabeth Sneddon, Esther Stephens, L. W. St. John, Seymour Wheelock, and Minnie Wilson.

The following libraries and research collections all contributed their fine staff assistance in various ways:

Cañon City Public Library Local History Center, Colorado Ski Museum and Hall of Fame, Delta County Historical Museum, Delta Public Library, Denver Public Library Western History Department, Garfield County Library (Parachute), Mesa County Public Library, Mary Reed Library of the University of Denver, Mesa State College Library, National Mining Hall of Fame (Leadville), Paonia Public Library, Savage Library at Western State College, and the Stephen Hart Library of the Colorado Historical Society.

Selected Bibliography

Reference works:

Encyclopedia Britannica
Marquis' *Who's Who in America* and *Who's Who* regional editions
Webster's International Biographical Dictionary
The International Who's Who
The People's Encyclopedia
Biographical Dictionary of the American Congress
Contemporary Authors
Who's Who in Art
Colorado, The Superstar State (Colorado Sports Hall of Fame)
Pratt Benagh's *Official Encyclopedia of Sports*

Specific books used in research were:

Evelyn I. Banning: *Helen Hunt Jackson*
Ed Blair: *Leadville, Colorado's Magic City*
Farrington Carpenter: *Confessions of a Maverick*
Helen Clapesattle: *Dr. Webb of Colorado Springs*
Mary Allen Converse: *Captain Mary*
Lyle Dorsett: *The Queen City, A History of Denver*
Amanda Ellis: *The Strange, Uncertain Years*
Elmer Ellis: *Henry Moore Teller*
David Even: *All the Years of American Popular Music*
Douglas Fairbanks: *Making Life Worthwhile*
Gene Fowler: *A Solo in Tom-Toms*
Michael Fromme: *Whose Woods These Are*
Leroy Hafen: *Colorado and Its People*
Frank Hall: *History of the State of Colorado*
Jack Kelly: *Koshare*
Harry Kelsey: *Frontier Capitalist*
Layton Kor: *Beyond the Vertical*
Robert W. Larson: *Shaping Educational Change*
Al Look: *Harold Bryant, Colorado's Maverick With a Paintbrush*
G. Michael McCarthy: *Hour of Trial*
Frances Melrose: *Rocky Mountain Memories*

John H. Monnett and G. Michael McCarthy: *Colorado Profiles*
George Norlin: *Things in the Saddle*
Len Shoemaker: *Saga of a Forest Ranger*
Jerome Smiley: *History of Denver*
Duane Smith: *Colorado Mining* and editor of *A Taste of the West*
H. Allen Smith: *To Hell in a Handbasket* and *The Life and Legend of Gene Fowler*
Wilbur Fisk Stone: *History of Colorado*
Ida Libert Uchill: *Pioneers, Peddlers and Tsaudium.*

Newspapers and Other Periodicals

Newspapers and other periodicals constituted a major source of reference. A multitude of nameless writers of obituaries deserve a note of particular gratitude. Some of these were in scrapbook clippings without source notes, but those identified included the following:

The Rocky Mountain News
The Denver Tribune
The Denver Post
The Grand Junction Daily Sentinel
The Pueblo Chieftain
Colorado Magazine
Colorado Heritage
Essays and Monographs in Colorado History (Colorado Historical Society)
Denver Westerners' Brand Books
Denver Westerners' Roundup
Spectrum (University of Northern Colorado)
and the Western Writers of America *Roundup*.

Two unpublished works should also be noted: Charles Livermore's doctoral dissertation at the University of Denver: *James G. Patton,* and Faith Stukey's graduate study at Western State College: *Edward Thomas Taylor.*

About the Author

Abbott Fay is a retired history professor who still teaches continuing education courses for three Colorado colleges. He has been involved with Colorado history for four and a half decades.

Now living near Paonia on the Western Slope of Colorado, he also leads historical tours and gives talks on history around the state. He has written four other books, the most recent being *Ski Tracks in the Rockies: A Century of Colorado Skiing*.

Your Suggestions Are Welcome!

Perhaps you believe that someone who deserved recognition in this book has been neglected.

The author had to select from nearly 200 suggestions. His standards were that the individual be born in Colorado or have made a substantial contribution to the activity for which he became famous while a resident of the state for a reasonable length time. Furthermore, the person must have gained lasting fame on a national, rather than regional or statewide, scale.

In spite of this, some subjective selection had to be made, and it is quite possible that an important person under these qualifications did not come to the attention of the writer.

You are invited to make suggestions for inclusion in a future edition of this work. Please write or telephone:

Abbott Fay
1750 Highway 133
Paonia, CO 81428
(303) 527-3120

Index

Individuals who are the subject of a full biography are shown in ALL CAPS; the pages of their biographies are shown in **boldface**.

D

Y

Z